YOUTHJOBS

Recent Titles from QUORUM BOOKS

YOUTHJOBS

Toward a
Private/Public
Partnership

DAVID BRESNICK

Foreword by
FRANK MACCHIAROLA

Q

QUORUM BOOKS
Westport, Connecticut
London, England

Library of Congress Cataloging in Publication Data

Bresnick, David.
   Youthjobs.

   Bibliography: p.
   Includes index.
   1. Youth—Employment—United States.   I. Title.
HD6273.B74   1984   331.3′412042′0973   84-3343
ISBN 0-89930-093-6 (lib. bdg.)

Library of Congress Catalog Card Number: 84-3343
ISBN: 0-89930-093-6

First published in 1984 by Quorum Books

Greenwood Press
A division of Congressional Information Service, Inc.
88 Post Road West, Westport, Connecticut 06881

Printed in the United States of America

10 9 8 7 6 5 4 3 2 1

To our youth and their too lonely struggle upstream.

Contents

Illustrations

Foreword

There has never been a reasonable and working relationship in the United States between programs in education and programs in employment and job training. And there has never been a coherent agreed upon policy regarding how schools, job trainers and employers should relate to one another.

Educators have historically seen employers as interested in taking youngsters out of school before their full educational development. They have seen business's interest as exploitive and they have resisted the intrusion of business into the school curriculum. For many years, within the setting of the American high school—save the vocational school—business subjects were downgraded, and the connection between schools and jobs was ignored.

This defensive response, developed when jobs were plentiful, was in keeping with the American dream of a college education for all who could survive high school. Indeed, the students who left school before the word "drop out" had meaning found jobs in industrial America. Several things have, however, begun to emerge over the last several decades that have changed a great deal of this. As America has moved into the post–industrialized era, we have seen the nature of jobs change. Many of the newer jobs have begun to require better academic skills. The high school diploma has become a job requirement as virtually every employer now wants his potential worker to be better prepared in school. But while employers have insisted on a better prepared high school graduate, the quality of public schooling in America has declined dramatically. Scores confirm what employers know: too many high school graduates can't read or write, or do simple math. What has made all of this more crushing to the young people is that as the need for skills has increased, and their level of skills has decreased, jobs have become more scarce. High unemployment levels in this country—concentrated among poor minority youngsters in America's cities—have given us a national crisis, and a profound challenge.

When we have addressed problems of youngsters without jobs, or youngsters without skills, analysts have put forward grand schemes to overhaul large parts of the service delivery systems. There have been many "full employment" proposals, many reform proposals to improve our nation's schools, and many proposals to overhaul job training programs. They generally have met with great resistance. "Full employment" gets in the way of other economic matters—like inflation and the cost of government. School reform that does more than pump additional dollars into school systems and that asks for more effective teacher and student output meets tremendous resistance from traditional providers. The policies of job training programs often guarantee that huge targets of those in need are ignored. Indeed, when dealing with our youth, it is important to remember how badly disenfranchised they actually are. Unlike those who deliver the service, youth recipients are unable to vote, and unable to strike. Their political participation is extremely limited because of lack of interest and a lack of training in the participatory process. American education has operated to conceal the meaning of democracy from its students. American students have, however, voted with their feet—leaving school at alarming rates and sending the drop out rate to pre–World War II levels. As a result, even with strong interest, and strong rhetoric about doing something about America's youth, we remain as a society unable to deliver two basic results that would be the products of effective education and job training: the guarantee of an education, and the guarantee of a job.

We remain unable to deliver on these guarantees because we have failed to appreciate how reluctant American society is to have grand solutions imposed upon us. We have assumed that government can do virtually all of what has to be done to help America's youth and we have assumed that government can do it well. We have forgotten that America's disrespect for expanded government is quite fundamental and that it is quite justified. More modest and more workable approaches are the most effective.

There are some approaches that would be helpful in the areas of employment, education and job training policy. In terms of employment policy, government, labor and business should make strong efforts to see that job opportunities for young people are promoted. This is not only the responsibility of the government, but it is also the responsibility of the employers themselves, individually and collectively. They should make the effort to tie our youngsters to the work place and government must invite the participation of the private sector. The partnership between government and business in promoting summer employment of disadvantaged youth in New York City under the New York City Partnership has been a shared responsibility for dealing with youth unemployment. Such a voluntary undertaking not only provides employment for youngsters, but it also serves to remind the private sector of an important responsibility to assure that our youngsters are being welcomed into the work force. Government's effort should be to provide incentives—tax credits, a reduced minimum wage—but it cannot go into the business of creating jobs for their own sake. Such jobs, poorly supervised and without real purpose for youngsters, give a totally dishonest picture of work. The employment opportunities when allowed to develop in the private sector—where they are real—are the ones that the government should sponsor.

In terms of educational policy, here too we have seen grand proposals that have suggested many changes in the curriculum and more hours per day and more days per year of instruction. The costs of the enhancements—including healthy salary increases—are considerable and in many respects the reforms have not drawn strong enough connections between jobs and school. Business must become involved in schools, lending expertise and advice in many areas, most importantly in areas of job development. Corporate involvement through the "join in a school" model, and through work study programs is an important part of the development of good school programs. In addition, there should be work done so that the school curriculum will include subjects that will assist students in learning the personal skills necessary to holding a job. The distance between how well students are prepared today and how prepared they must be to maintain a job are great. Even such matters as student dress, work habits, attendance and lateness require the attention of school reformers. It goes without saying that standards for promotion and graduation must also be addressed. Schools must develop these standards in concert with business and not be afraid to hold back students who are not able to meet the standards for the first time. The overriding lesson of the school reform literature is that the quality of our educational system is not yet adequate to the task of meeting the challenge of this century and the next.

In terms of job training, here again grand schemes should give way to more modest—and workable—proposals. The job training effort, when sponsored by government, should focus upon entry level jobs for youngsters who have not succeeded in school. The government must respond to those least able to help themselves—drop outs, ex–offenders, ex–drug addicts—those who must travel in many cases great distances if they are to get and keep their first job. Private enterprise can focus on developing the connection between jobs in the primary and secondary job markets. But if job training programs succeed in getting entry level jobs for these disadvantaged youngsters the result will be a meaningful, even if modest contribution.

Jobs for young people are not easily secured as the history of job training and youth employment programs demonstrate. There is, moreover, no way that they can be attained for most young people if we rely upon government, and if we expect government programs to replace our own resolve. More modest approaches—which encourage private sector involvement, and which involve programs that can work—will in the long run be more effective in connecting our youngsters to society.

Frank J. Macchiarola

Preface

My interest in youth unemployment, its consequences and its cures, has two origins. For several years I worked at the New York City Board of Education where I became familiar with the frustrations attendant to vocational education. And I became interested in employment and training programs, including youth programs intended to aid disadvantaged youth. As I searched for the causes and consequences of youth unemployment, I became convinced that there was a problem and a solution. I believe we are shortchanging our youth, especially those not going on to college, by providing those needing the most help in entering the job market with the least assistance. I also believe that our companies are losing out, but that the larger society is the greater loser, having to bear the brunt of the social dislocation resulting from youth unemployment.

I owe a debt to a number of individuals who by sharing their insights helped build my own perspective. From my days at the Board of Education Seymour Lachman and Murray Polner helped assimilate and critically appraise the shortcomings of secondary education and vocational education in particular. Joe Ball has been a constant foil in our discussions of vocational education and employment and training policy since our graduate school days. Beatrice Reubens alerted me early in the study to some of the complexities of apprenticeship on an international scale. Paul Barton confirmed my own optimism about the prospects for doing more for our youth.

Jarl Bengtsson facilitated my contact with the Organization for Economic Cooperation and Development and its outstanding staff. His insight and those of others, especially Chris Brooks, have profoundly influenced my treatment of European comparisons. A host of other individuals have extended my understanding. Particular thanks are due Birgitta Ahlkvist of the Swedish Employers' Confederation and Ingrid Drexel of the Institut fur Sozialwissenschafliche in Munich.

YOUTHJOBS

CHAPTER 1

The Youth Labor Market

THE EXTENT OF YOUTH UNEMPLOYMENT

Since the 1950s teenage unemployment in the United States has been rising and has passed several plateaus. In the mid–1950s the teenage unemployment rate rose above 10 percent. Until 1970 it fluctuated between 10 percent and 17 percent. Since October 1981, it has remained above 20 percent, setting a new record almost every month. The teenage unemployment rate for the second quarter of 1983 was 23.9 percent. Teenage unemployment for the same period in New York City was 34.8 percent.

Of course, the rate of teenage unemployment or youth unemployment does not rise on its own but follows adult unemployment, which has remained above 8 percent since October 1981. Since the 1950s, adult unemployment has fluctuated up and down—as recently as 1979 it was at 5.8 percent—while teenage unemployment has assumed an increasing spiral.

A general rise in adult and youth unemployment rates has also taken place in the other advanced industrialized countries, especially since the 1974–1975 recession.[1] By 1975, teenage unemployment in the United States reached nearly 20 percent, while the next highest industrialized countries were Italy and Canada, ranging between 15 and 17 percent. French and British teenagers for the first time experienced unemployment rates exceeding 10 percent. German and Japanese unemployment still remained quite low at 4.7 percent and 3.7 percent each. By 1978 and 1979, teenage unemployment in France, Great Britain, and Italy all exceeded that in the United States at some point. Germany and Japan still remained below 5 percent, while Sweden's ranged from 5.5 to 8.2 percent between 1975 and 1980. More recently teenage unemployment has continued to rise. Except in Japan, youth have borne a growing share of total unemployment since 1960.

While the United States has been providing more and more jobs, the rate of youth unemployment keeps climbing. European countries were helped by a fall in the rate of labor participation by the young, as larger numbers began attending upper secondary school. During the 1960s, tight labor markets and strong economies in Europe and Japan resulted in high demand for young workers. Labor shortages increased the access of young people to jobs. In Japan, the United Kingdom, and Germany, employers actively recruited youth from schools and were willing to provide additional training. But in countries like France, Italy, and the United States, active youth recruitment did not occur.

What are the prospects for the future? Under projections by the U.S. Bureau of Labor Statistics, the numbers of teenagers in the work force should drop after 1985 and result by 1995 in a reduction of approximately 10 percent in that portion of the labor force. Certainly the labor market should be better able to cope with a reduction than it has in the past with an increase. But some observers point out that given increased competition from other groups, such as women reentering work and continued changes in the youth labor market, things may be even more difficult. The agricultural and industrial sectors, which have provided most jobs for youth, are scheduled to experience further contractions.

The current precipitous rise in the youth unemployment rate has reinforced the arguments of some that the problem of youth unemployment deserves special attention. A youth labor market that behaves differently from the adult labor market may require special remedies.

THE TRANSITIONAL NATURE OF YOUTH UNEMPLOYMENT

Why is it that so many teenagers who are seeking employment are unemployed? Why must many continue in school only because no job is available? Meanwhile others who would prefer full-time work can only find part-time work. And some are discouraged by their failure to obtain work and no longer seek employment.

The major factor, as we have already recognized, is the overall weakness of the labor market. Teenagers tend to be at the end of the line of those considered for a job. The outstanding fact of youth unemployment is that every youth group has a higher unemployment rate than every non-youth group when divided according to other characteristics such as sex and occupation. The last in line will always be those individuals and groups considered to be least desirable: the young, the poorly educated, and minorities. Employers resist hiring young workers: they do not have extensive experience; they do not have the personal contacts acquired by activity in the labor market; and they are regarded as unreliable and irresponsible.

Perhaps the major distinguishing characteristic of the youth labor market in particular is the fact that so many individuals are entering the labor market for the first time. This means that the rate of unemployment for the group as a whole will be abnormally high. A related factor is the short duration of many job experiences of the young. Teenagers and even those in their twenties experience a succession of jobs of short duration. They change jobs and move in and out of the labor force with much greater frequency than any other group. This contributes to an overall instability in employment. In part this reflects dissatisfaction with low pay and minimal work. As Martin Feldstein, the head of the President's Council of Economic Advisors, argues, a necessary component of any policy aimed at reducing teenage unemployment is promoting employment stability among young workers.[2] This point of view is supported by the findings of others such as Parnes and Kohen that job immobility is strongly associated with the avoidance of unemployment.[3] They suggest that a real advantage lies with those who find satisfactory initial jobs and remain in them.

The temporary nature of many youth jobs is reinforced by the phenomenon of part-time work. An increasing proportion of young people are holding part-time jobs, while they attend school. In 1967, for example, 14 million 16–17 year olds were engaged in voluntary part-time work. Only 455,000 were working full time. Recent data indicated that 50 percent of those between 16 and 19 attending school were also working at least part time. This compares with 75 percent labor force participation among those not attending school. Another interesting fact is that the unemployment rate for those out of school exceeds that for those in school, again perhaps indicating that the youth job market now caters to in-school youth more than out-of-school youth.

The difficulties that youth experience in entering the job market upon graduation from high school are confirmed by a recent analysis of data from the National Longitudinal Survey of the High School Class of 1972 (NLS).[4] Of those who chose not to go on for further education, in effect those choosing to enter the labor market, only 27.7 percent had lined up jobs to begin work by June 1, the date taken as roughly equivalent to graduation. An additional 55.4 percent expected to begin work between September 1 and January 1, and the remaining 5.2 percent anticipated starting work after January 1, 1973. Those actually indicating that they were employed as of June 1 were 49.4 percent, including those who were continuing part-time jobs begun while in high school. Additional labor market data was obtained as of October 1972 and October

1973 for this group. Overall, 70.8 percent were working full time by October 1972, 9.4 percent were working part time, 8.3 percent were unemployed, and 11.5 percent had removed themselves from the labor force. One year later in October 1973, 75.2 percent indicated they were working full time, 5.8 percent indicated they were working part time, 6.6 percent indicated they were unemployed, while 12.3 percent indicated they were out of the labor force.

Nearly 30 percent of the class of 1972 had not obtained full-time jobs by October 1972, and nearly 25 percent had not obtained full-time jobs by October 1973. While only 8.3 percent in 1972 and 6.6 percent in 1973 indicated they were actively seeking employment, the number who were discouraged, not working full time, or back in school because they could not find work was probably closer to 20 percent.

A SECONDARY LABOR MARKET

The transitional and temporary nature of the youth job market has been observed for a long time. At least since the early 1950s it has been recognized that young persons are seldom in employment on a regular basis before the age of 20 years. High unemployment for youth is characteristic of good times and bad. But as late as the 1960s it was believed that the teenage labor market was highly flexible and closely interrelated to the adult labor market and that the employability of teenagers was not impaired by increased minimum wages or technological changes. Recently greater attention has been given to describing the special characteristics of the youth labor market.

Marcia Freedman analyzed the American labor market in 1960 and 1970, dividing it into 16 and 14 segments, respectively, based upon type of occupation, industry, and earnings level.[5] She found that young workers were underrepresented in all 6 of the top segments both in 1960 and 1970. Younger workers began to increase their representation around segment 5. By segment 11, they were overrepresented and remained so in most of the rest of the groups.

Her investigations noted great differences between youth below 20 and those above 20. Part-time work represents an important element in youth employment, which is closely related to schooling. In 1970, while only 4 percent of mature men and 23 percent of mature women held part-time jobs, 31 percent of young workers held part-time jobs.

She found that the work experience of teenagers is random and irrelevant to the jobs they hold in later life. Starting at about 20, those who work full time enter upon a transition period that sets the stage for their occupational futures. Movement out of the youth labor market is signaled by increasing job tenure and declining unemployment rates. Median time on the job, which is 7 months for teenage workers, doubles to 14 months for those 20 to 24.

Paul Osterman studied a group of 150 non-college young men in the Boston communities of East Boston and Roxbury in an attempt to understand how young people enter the job market.[6] He found that when young people leave high school they are generally not prepared for stable, reliable, full-time positions. He found that jobs young people hold in their early years are usually casual and unskilled. Osterman adopts Michael Piore's distinction between primary and secondary markets in characterizing this youth job market as secondary. These jobs may be located in "mom and pop" stores, "under the table" arrangements, or large firms. The jobs are often obtained on a "walk-in" basis and are at or close to the minimum wage. Osterman categorizes this period before graduation to the primary labor market as the moratorium period for youth, when sex, adventure, and peer group activities are more important than work. Entry into the labor market occurs in stages and requires time, so that employers are justified in not viewing younger workers as career employees. A secondary labor market is thus created for youth until it matures.

Primary labor market jobs are provided by firms that offer stable, long-term jobs with reasonable opportunity for promotion and advancement and with well-articulated internal labor markets. Osterman finds that these firms are more interested in reliability, maturity, and ability to learn than past knowledge. Virtually every firm interviewed cited attitude as the central consideration in hiring.

A recognition that the segmentation of the labor market is due in part to the attitude of many businessmen that youth are inferior to older workers has been buttressed by a number of studies. One of the earliest studies, during the 1960s, focused on Detroit companies. It found that 40 percent of all employers (100 or more employees) accounted for 55 percent of all office and retail jobs of those between 16 and 21. The larger the company the more likely they were to have available entry-level positions. Perhaps even more significant was the lack of willingness to hire 16–21 year olds. Of 35,091 Detroit businessmen, 38 percent said they had entry-level jobs that could be filled by ages 16–21. Only 26 percent indicated a disposition to hire youth, and only 10 percent actually did hire them. A majority of employers and, according to some, as many as 80 percent of all employers do not want to hire young people for regular jobs until the age of 21. According to Barton, regardless of employment or unemployment statistics, the reality for high school graduates is thus not much different than for dropouts.

A study conducted by the Manpower Institute in 1973 used intensive interviewing of executives to probe their attitudes.[7] It found little empirical basis for these attitudes and little willingness on the part of the employers to test their working hypothesis. Nor have business executives perceived youth unemployment as a salient issue. On the other hand, some companies do hire large numbers of youth. A study of three

large companies found that between 35 and 47 percent of the new hir-
ees were youth between the ages of 15 and 21,[8] that hiring of minority
youth was substantial, and that a high school diploma was an asset.
By and large this study found no difference between the performance
of these young workers and older workers in similar jobs.

Paul Barton has studied the reluctance of primary firms to hire young
workers, which forces youth into the secondary sector, where their
natural tendencies toward unstable behavior are reinforced.[9] He argues
that this hiring pattern on the part of primary firms is the central determinant of the youth labor market, and not, as is frequently argued,
the youngster's lack of entry-level skills. Several commentators find that
the gap between teenage and adult employment is traceable to the
nonpathological characteristics of teenagers and their interaction with
societal institutions, which view them in a disparaging way and make
it difficult for them to move from school to work.

As most of the academically capable youth go on to college, the quality of those remaining is perceived as reduced. Another commentator
states that the problem of youth joblessness appears to be due to the
lack of jobs rather than to poor work attitudes or unrealistic salaries.
The high mobility and short tenure of the young, shaped by the character of the youth labor market, make unemployment an ever present
danger.

As Barton argues, however, it is not so much the rate of youth unemployment that is the problem as the fact of the youth labor market.
For those attending higher education it works well. They are not interested in career positions and are able to find temporary jobs that provide income and work experience. But for those teenagers who seek
full-time work leading to career stability, the outlook is bleak. They enter an enforced period of job instability and change. To those who have
probably already experienced the insecurities of poor performance in
secondary school, such experiences are not calculated to bring attachment to the society and a smooth entrance into the world of work.

THE IMPLICATIONS OF THE YOUTH LABOR MARKET

For those youth who attend college, the youth labor market of part-
time, temporary jobs works well. It is suited to their needs as students
and future workers in helping ease their transition to full-time work upon
graduation from college. During their college years it provides limited
income and work experience. The implications for school leavers not
planning to attend college, however, are different. For those students
who pursue full-time employment rather than completing college, it has
made securing career employment more difficult. In a job market, where
the median duration of jobs for youth is 7 months and 14 months for

those youth over 20, the opportunities for developing attachment to an organization and developing job skills are minimal.

The transitional and temporary nature of the youth labor market has been observed for a long time. One observer writing in the late 1960s observed, "Teenagers have always been more susceptible to unemployment than adults."[10] He rejected the contention, however, that the structure of the labor market was changing so that it was becoming more difficult to obtain entry-level positions leading to career opportunities. More teenagers than ever were employed. The problem was that not enough new jobs were created to meet the demand for an expanding labor force.

By the 1980s, however, this refrain has begun to wear thin, as youth unemployment rates continue to soar. There is an increasing recognition that the growth in the service sector as opposed to the industrial and farm sectors has hurt youth disproportionately. Some argue that the decrease in agricultural demand for labor has been a major factor in increasing youth unemployment since the 1950s, particularly among nonwhite youth. The movement away from agriculture has resulted in a decline in relative importance of unskilled jobs.

Projections indicate that trends will continue to hurt the prospects for employing youth. Furthermore, there is an increasing recognition that career entry positions for teenagers have virtually disappeared. Data from the National Longitudinal Survey indicate that high school employment and first jobs held upon leaving school tend to be in the secondary labor market. The jobs can be learned rapidly and provide little in the way of job-related skills that can be used subsequently.[11] Certainly the large corporations are recruiting their career employees in the mid-twenties. No doubt the widespread growth of college attendance has contributed to this phenomenon. With large portions and certainly a higher proportion of the most qualified young people attending college, it is not surprising that companies have adapted their hiring practices. One explanation for the rise in youth unemployment is the loss of relative quality in those entering the job market now that so many go on to college.

While the temporary, insecure nature of the youth labor market probably serves the college-bound well, its helpfulness for those seeking full-time career positions is less certain. For the small group of low-educated (often minority) youngsters for whom youth employment is a special problem, its effects are devastating. The problem faced by this small but significant group is that the jobs that traditionally were open to them in industry that required their physical stamina are increasingly disappearing.

Robert Lehrman made some calculations regarding those youth who were unemployed for 15 weeks or longer.[12] He found that out of a total youth unemployment of 2,865,000, 2,326,000 were out of school and presumably seeking full-time employment, while only 539,000 were students. Of those out of school, 785,000 had not completed high school.

These numbers do not include those who were enrolled in school but not working and those who may be discouraged from seeking work, or those who were looking for work less than 15 weeks, or those who may have part-time jobs but are seeking full-time work. That number was surely over 3 million and could easily have reached 5 million. The results of this shortfall in jobs is skyrocketing unemployment rates for youth 16–24, with particular emphasis on the group between 16 and 19, and especially minority youth.

By and large the youth contending for full-time jobs are those individuals who have "dropped out" from the educational system and given up the schools as a source of socialization and personal attachment. Unless they obtain employment, these young people will have no regular attachment to a socializing institution. To the extent that these youth do not obtain productive jobs, they lose personal income and represent a loss to the larger society. They also present additional potential social problems. While this group appears to be quite small, they nonetheless account for a substantial portion of total teenage unemployment and present considerable potential problems.

Given the changes that have been described in the youth labor market, it seems unlikely that the fall-off in young workers will prove self-correcting. Even with the projected decrease in young people entering the labor market over the next 20 years, the shortage of career positions for school leavers promises to stay with us. All involuntary joblessness represents a loss of real output for society as well as a loss of income for the individual. Even if individual businesses can sustain themselves in a surplus labor market, the loss to the society as a whole is not tolerable. It is doubtful that even a country as prosperous as the United States can afford to forgo the productive capacity of so large a group of its population. From a social policy perspective, the relegation of a significant proportion of our population to marginal employment and continuing periods of unemployment has profound consequences. It means the society must be willing to absorb the social welfare costs of this group. It also means we must be willing to sanction the existence of an underclass of temporary workers who have no real hope of becoming integrated into the mainstream of our society.

Apart from the potential anti-social behavior of youth unable to obtain jobs, a larger issue is whether society is justified in denying young people the opportunity to partake in adult society. We may prefer to pretend that youth have not arrived to adulthood. Yet clearly youth is strong enough and able enough and knows enough to engage in many forms of work. Ball has suggested that we should be prepared to allow

13 year olds to begin varying their educational diet with one day per week of work and that by age 15 three days a week should be permitted.[13]

The quest for greater employment opportunities for youth may be conceived, then, as an attempt to provide greater choice in the society, particularly if entry into the labor market is viewed as a positive good, not one that takes on greater value the longer it can be deferred. The situation in the youth labor market today is different from what it was in the 1950s and earlier.[14] Yet our approach to preparing young people for the labor market is based upon an earlier view. In fact, the roots of our current approach are in the American secondary school system and its vocational education aspects, which were formed in the first part of the twentieth century. An understanding of our current dilemma presupposes an understanding of how our schools prepare our youth for the world of work.

NOTES

1. The comparative statistical picture is presented by Constance Sorrentino, "Youth Unemployment: An International Perspective," *Monthly Labor Review* 104, (1981): 3–14. Comparative youth unemployment data are regularly published by the Organization for Economic Cooperation and Development (OECD).

2. Martin Feldstein, "The Economics of the New Unemployment," *Public Interest*, no. 33 (1973): 3–42.

3. Herbert Parnes and Andrew Kohen, "Labor Market Experience of Noncollege Youth: A Longitudinal Analysis," in *From School to Work* (Washington, D.C.: National Commission for Manpower Policy, 1976).

4. George Nolfi et al., *Experiences of Recent High School Graduates* (Lexington, Mass.: Heath, 1978).

5. Marcia Freedman, *Labor Markets: Segments and Shelters* (Montclair, N.J.: Allanheld, Osmun, 1976).

6. Paul Osterman, *Getting Started: The Youth Labor Market* (Cambridge, Mass.: MIT Press, 1980).

7. Manpower Institute, *Study of Corporate Youth Employment Policies and Practices* (Washington, D.C.: Manpower Institute, 1973).

8. Fred Cook and Frank Lanhan, "Opportunities and Requirements for Initial Employment of School Leavers with Emphasis on Office and Retail Jobs" (Ph.D. diss., Wayne State University, 1966).

9. Paul Barton, "Youth Transition to Work," in *From School to Work* (Washington, D.C.: National Commission for Manpower Policy, 1976), p. 3.

10. Edward Kalchek, *The Youth Labor Market* (Washington, D.C.: National Manpower Policy Task Force, 1969).

11. Wayne Stevenson, "The Transition from School to Work," in *The Lingering Crisis of Youth Unemployment*, ed. Arvil V. Adams and Garth L. Mangum. (Kalamazoo, Mich.: W. E. Upjohn Institute for Employment Research, 1978).

12. Robert Lehrman, "An Analysis of Youth Employment Problems," in *A*

Review of Youth Employment Problems, Programs and Policies, by U.S. Vice President's Task Force on Youth Employment, Vol. 1 (Washington, D.C.: Government Printing Office, 1980).

13. Colin Ball and Meg Ball, *Fit For Work?* (London: Writers and Readers, 1979).

14. For projections of the future job market for youth, *see* B. G. Reubens, J.A.C. Harrisson, and K. Rupp, *The Youth Labor Force 1945–1955: A Cross-National Analysis* (Totowa, N.J.: Allanheld, Osmun, 1981).

CHAPTER 2

Vocational Education American Style

THE DEVELOPMENT OF THE SYSTEM

After World War II, when the American economy was booming, American vocational education was looked upon with great favor throughout the world. As unemployment rose and the economy slowed down during the 1970s and 1980s, vocational education was denigrated by foreign and domestic critics. It is fashionable today to cite the graduates of vocational education programs who cannot find jobs, the inadequacies of graduates and dropouts from the American high school, and the difficulty that vocational education has in keeping up with the changing economy and the changing nature of work. Yet when the American high school developed and its vocational component was strengthened by the Smith-Hughes Act of 1917, it represented a progressive break with the past. That legislation was made possible when the American Federation of Labor and the National Association of Manufacturers dropped their earlier opposition and supported the inclusion of vocational education within the public schools.

The importance of this decision extended beyond the individuals who would be given an opportunity to pursue vocational training before leaving secondary school. The effect of the decision was to deemphasize the role of employers in the initial training of young workers. Labor viewed vocational education in the schools as a way of reducing the competition between adult workers and young workers, and the general public was pleased to remove the young from the vulnerabilities of child labor.

Those attending vocational schools remained a small percentage of the total number of young people remaining in school, but they reinforced the view that young people should stay in school as long as possible. In a review of vocational educational practice conducted for the Organization for Economic Cooperation and Development in 1967, the effects of this policy were noted. In the United States, 75 percent of the relevant age groups were obtaining high school certificates, as opposed to 7–15 percent in European countries. Yet the report cited statistics showing that only 2.3 percent of the 15–19 age group were taking courses preparing them for industry and commerce. At the same time the report noted that only 7 percent of company employees benefited from training organized by companies, and most of these were managers or technicians. In fact, the report made the following startling statement: "The example of the United States therefore gives cause for thought. That country's technical progress and economic growth has been achieved in the absence of any genuine vocational education."[1]

Let us use that statement as a departure to investigate the special character of the American high school, its contribution to American success, and why it is still emulated today.

The belief in education as part of the democratic ideal is an important dimension of American ideology. Even before the American Revolution there were more degree-granting institutions in America than in Great Britain. By 1830 the school-enrolled portion of the population in the United States was second only to Germany. By 1850 there was little doubt that the U.S. population was the best educated in the world.[2] This was in large part due to the common school, which covered the primary years. In subsequent years the proportion of the population attending school rose, reaching 22 percent by 1887 and 24 percent by 1928. Its closest competitor in 1928 was Ireland, with 18 percent of its population in school.

From the earliest times, controversy centered on the role of vocational education in the high school. In the earliest legislation, adopted in the state of Massachusetts in 1827, every town of more than 500 families was required to have a high school that would teach U.S. history, bookkeeping, algebra, geometry, and surveying, while every town with at least 4,000 inhabitants was required to offer instruction in Greek, Latin, history, rhetoric, and logic. This resulted in an early distinction between the so-called English schools, emphasizing more practical subjects, and the classic schools, offering more traditional education. Independent institutions focusing on vocational training grew up outside of the public high schools. Yet most of those established prior to the Civil War did not survive. A combination of factors undermined the vocational schools, including rich agricultural conditions, which did not seem to need scientific management, and the identification of vocational education with culturally inferior education. Vocational education was considered second-class education, detracting from the democratic, uplifting functions of the high schools.

Yet despite this uncertain support for vocational education at the secondary school level, the Morrill Act of 1862 gave a strong boost to vocational and technical education at the university level. By establishing the land grant colleges, it created a network of agricultural and technical universities across the country that became the cornerstone of American industrial and agricultural success. It also served to legitimize technical and vocational education, making them more acceptable for introduction into the secondary schools.

The introduction of vocational education into secondary education, which was greatly stimulated by the Smith-Hughes Act of 1917, was part of an international movement that is sometimes referred to as the manual training movement. American interest was first spurred by the World's Fair in London in 1851, which demonstrated the high level of application of science to industry in Europe. Massachusetts businessmen who attended were influential in supporting legislation that first created industrial and mechanical drawing as a subject of study in the schools, then made it compulsory, and then created the Massachusetts Normal Art School to train teachers in this subject. In 1872, the Swedish government contributed to this international movement by introducing manual training into all schools to counteract the bad physical and moral effects of city living and to help revitalize industry. Special schools were created to train teachers for these schools.

But the event that more than any propelled vocational education forward in the United States was the Philadelphia Centennial exposition of 1876. The exhibit that attracted particular attention was that of the Russian use of "instruction" shops for teaching manual trades. John D. Runkle, the president of the Massachusetts Institute of Technology, saw in the Russian approach an alternative to the faltering apprenticeship system. His report led to the creation of a school of the mechanical arts. Other privately supported schools sprung up throughout the country. Soon the public schools began incorporating similar programs. When in the late 1880s Massachusetts adopted legislation requiring every city over 25,000 to provide manual training in the high schools, it already could be found in most public schools. In some cases it became part of the general curriculum, while in others it became a separate course of study within the high school. In some schools it became a separate program, often requiring a longer day of instruction.

As the manual training movement became rooted in the high schools as well as within the proprietary schools, it spearheaded a major shift in the role of the American high school. From a preparatory school for those attending university it became a terminal school for those entering the labor market. In 1900, 6 percent of all young people completed high school, rising to 17 percent by 1920. After World War II, over 70 percent completed high school. In 1870, 80 percent of the high school graduates entered college and 60 percent obtained college degrees. By 1940 only 15 percent of the high school graduates received college degrees.

In the period after World War II, the rate of attendance at secondary school, already at a high level, remained stable, while the level of those attending postsecondary school increased dramatically until the 1970s, when it leveled off. By 1929–30, 51.3 percent of 14–17 year olds were attending high school; by 1939–40 it was 73.3 percent; and by 1959–60 it was 83.2 percent. Also of note was the development of the public higher educational system and the rapid explosion of the two-year colleges.

During the latter part of the nineteenth century traditionalism reasserted itself. After encouraging the development of the manual training movement, the National Education Association criticized it as endangering the liberal tradition, focusing on the importance of intelligence. Others saw vocational education as a poor substitute for classical education. Even its proponents, like John Dewey, criticized the direction that vocational education was taking, apart from general education. Dewey urged an integration of vocational education into general education. High school principals became more concerned with the ideology of foreign students than their vocational training. In many schools vocational education languished under poor support and inadequate and outdated resources.

By 1900, the American business community was concerned that the public schools were not capable of providing adequate vocational and technical education. In 1899 Theodore Search, president of the National Association of Manufacturers, argued that industrial education was essential if the United States were to compete successfully on world markets. The Douglas Commission, established by the Massachusetts legislature, focused attention on the need for industrial education and the inadequacy of the schools, which remained too literary. Manual training, too, was criticized for being too removed from life and giving too narrow a view. Its calls for the creation of independent industrial schools gave impetus to the creation of the National Society for the Promotion of Industrial Education, which performed an important advocacy role.

By 1910, both the American Federation of Labor and the National Association of Manufacturers had dropped their earlier opposition and backed the inclusion of vocational education within the public schools. In 1917 the Smith-Hughes Act resulted in substantial federal funding of vocational education programs across the country.

VOCATIONAL EDUCATION AND THE COMPREHENSIVE HIGH SCHOOL

The Smith-Hughes Act of 1917 provided $7.2 million for state vocational education programs. Additional monies were provided by the George-Dean Act of 1936 and its replacement, the George-Barden Act of 1946, which authorized an additional $29 million for vocational education programs. With the election of President John F. Kennedy in 1960, the American Vocational Association, representing educators and professionals from throughout the country, undertook a concerted effort to obtain additional federal funding. With the support of HEW Secretary Abraham Ribicoff, a high-level study group chaired by Benjamin Willis, superintendent of the Chicago Public Schools, was appointed. The group recommended a large increase in federal expenditures for vocational education and the abolition of the specific targeted categories of vocational education contained in the Smith-Hughes and George-Barden Acts. The study group's recommendations were incorporated into the Vocational Education Act of 1963. Area vocational schools (referred to as AVSs or AVTSs) grew dramatically so that by 1975 there were over 2,452 of these institutions. They are ordinarily either independent secondary schools or departments of comprehensive schools. Some are organized differently to serve those who have left school. They are required to provide vocational education to no less than five different occupational fields for those preparing full time for labor market entry.

But even as the Vocational Education Act of 1963 was passed, its efficacy was being questioned and challenged by the passage of the Manpower Development and Training Act of 1962 (MDTA). Described fully in the next chapter, MDTA was administered by the Department of Labor, which built a competing model of preparation for work, first by focusing on workers displaced by automation and later on the disadvantaged, who were having difficulty finding jobs. In addition to providing classroom training, MDTA provided a model for on-the-job training (OJT) on the employer's premises.

As long as unemployment remained low and the system resulted in relatively open and stable employment, indeed, job mobility for millions of Americans, its success seemed indisputable. The American high school with its vocational education component seemed unassailable. But as youth unemployment grew in the 1960s and 1970s, the system received increasing criticism. The irony may be, however, that in a time of economic boom such as the immediate post–World War II period, any system and particularly a flexible system will work well. Companies eager for new employees will hire from the available labor supply and may not be too critical of the quality of the supply. They will eagerly accept young workers as well as more experienced ones.

But during the period of the 1960s, even as the Congress was demonstrating its commitment to our comprehensive system of education and its vocational education component, the premises of this generalized system of comprehensive education were being called into question. During the period up to World War II, the secondary school increasingly became a place for universal education, and most individuals entered the world of work directly from secondary school, whether or not they graduated. The rise in the proportion of the population attending secondary school and the lowering of the percentages that went on and graduated college reflected this new role.

This trend was not altered by the continuing federal support of vocation education. While the number of students in vocational education programs increased under stimulus from federal funding, most of the programs remained within comprehensive schools. This American phenomenon of the general secondary school was emulated to some extent by every other country included in this study in the period after World War II.

As the techniques of mass production were introduced and the dimensions of business shifted to require financial, creative, sales, and interpersonal skills, the graduates of these secondary schools, were prepared with a generalist education. Where specific skill training was needed it could be provided on the job, by the limited number of apprenticeship programs that remained, or by the influx of skilled workers from Europe. So that while the skill-based training that vocational education sought to emulate was never very successful, the new American approach to a general education provided the basic skills of literacy, communication, and creativity that were needed in so many aspects of business.

In this sense the system fulfilled the expectations of corporate leadership, which sought through vocational education to develop a wide range of personnel to man the new corporate industrial structure. Not only production workers were required but supervisors, technicians, and managers as well. Thus the elite American secondary school was transformed between 1890 and 1930 to a school for followers as well as leaders. The task of secondary school now became to help each student to find an appropriate place within the expanded curriculum and ultimately within the industrial society.[3] This also involved a socialization function in teaching all students how to work in large organizations and to accept the limitations of a complex society.[4] Tyack has characterized this development as the emergence of the high school as the people's college, a trend that was influenced by the early development of the common school and its democratic ideology.[5] In time, of course, the democratization of the high school would lead to the democratization of the college, too. Meanwhile, higher-level technical training was provided by institutions of higher education that had developed under the stimulus of the Morrill Act of 1862.

VOCATIONAL EDUCATION FOREIGN STYLE

In the period after World War II, while upper secondary school attendance in the United States remained stable at 70 percent, upper secondary school in other industrialized countries remained, for the most part, limited to those intending to go on to universities. To help fill the gap, specialized/vocational education programs developed. Since the 1960s the general educational facilities have expanded. The countries that have followed the United States most closely are Japan and Sweden. In fact, Japan has outdone the United States, so that by 1977 93 percent of those leaving lower secondary school entered upper secondary schools.

Sweden

Sweden provides a particularly interesting example because it had a system of education that was typical of Europe, including comprehensive education at the primary level and specialized vocational education at the secondary level.[6] However, in the post–World War II period they have progressively moved to a system that today looks very much like that of the United States.

Immediately following World War II, in 1945, 90 percent of Swedish young people attended school for at least 7 years, until the age of 14. Then, with the exception of the 20 percent who had begun to attend the Realskola, which lasted until age 16, the remaining group entered the labor force. Some of these entered vocational school. Then in 1948 school attendance for 7 years, from ages 7 to 14 was made compulsory, while some communities extended primary education to 8 years. In 1950 the Swedish Parliament extended compulsory schooling to 9 years, to take place in a comprehensive school, divided into junior, middle, and senior levels. Under this system a conscious effort was made to have all pupils follow the same courses and defer vocational choices until the end of the 9-year period, at the age of 17. By 1955 the primary schools had been converted to comprehensive schools with 100 percent attendance, and comprehensive lower secondary schools with vocation streams had been established. Seventy percent of those up to the age of 16 remained to completion. By 1965 compulsory education had been extended through the eighth year, with 90 percent of all students completing the ninth year. By 1975 the 9-year compulsory education had been attained, while 80 percent of all young people remained in school until the age of 18, attending comprehensive upper secondary school. In the upper secondary school, although it remains comprehensive, students pursue studies in one of three sectors: arts and social subjects; economics and commercial subjects; and scientific and technical subjects. Almost half of the students pursue vocationally oriented lines, intended to prepare students for the labor force, while the other half pursue academic lines leading to further study.

France

In contrast to Sweden, France has continued to rely on distinct vocational schools, which were introduced after 1959.[7] In France compulsory primary education was introduced in 1882 for those between the ages of 6 and 11. Secondary education remained optional and subject to fees. It led to the *baccalauréat*, which afforded access to higher education. In the period prior to World War I most workers entered the labor force without any vocational training. On-the-job training predominated. Exceptions were the few remaining apprenticeships, which continued to decline, a few "factory schools" created by major industrial concerns, and systems of vocational education, which never were too successful and were always considered inferior to the general education system. The Astier Law of July 25, 1919, required communal authorities to set up free vocational training courses for apprentices and young salaried workers during working hours. As a result of World War II, vocational training centers were established.

But in 1959, following the extension of compulsory schooling from age 14 to 16, several well-defined vocational and technical alternatives were introduced under the Ministry of Education. Outstanding among these were the *collèges d'enseignement technique* (CETs) to train young skilled workers and employees, and the *lycées techniques* to train technicians. At the same time training courses were organized for adult workers to provide occupational and engineering qualifications. A variety of reforms were introduced in 1966.

The *instituts universitaires de technologie (IUTs)* were established to undertake short-term advanced vocational training for senior technicians. And state responsibility for training was clarified, while coordination among government, business and trade union officials was enhanced by the creation of the National Council for Vocational Training. In July 1975, the Haby reform required manual and technical skills training for all children until the completion of the first cycle of secondary education.

While the rise in youth unemployment in France during the 1960s led to a series of Pactes Nationaux pour l'Emploi, providing training places in the private sector, the primary focus remains how to reinforce and improve the system of vocational education. The problem of youth unemployment is seen as particularly related to the school dropout, who is seen as the failure in the system. There is near unanimity of opinion among all the political parties that the need is to convince youth to remain in the school system and attain higher qualifications.

Despite the support for specialized vocational schools, France, like Sweden, has been moving toward a system of comprehensive education. The Haby reforms abolished the vocational education streams that had developed at the lower secondary schools. Those students who intend to leave school at age 16, however, may enroll in pre-apprenticeship courses as well as obtain some specialized vocational training while in lower secondary school. Graduates of the lower secondary schools may attend the *lycées d'enseignement professionnelle* (LEPs) for the short cycle of two years. This cycle leads to either the *certificat d'aptitude professionnelle* (CAP), which is specific to some skilled or white collar occupation, or to the *brevet d'études professionnelles* (BEP), which is a general vocational certificate.

Those attending the three-year cycle at the *lycées d'enseignement générale et technologique* can take the general course leading to the baccalaureate and further education; the technical course leading to the *brevet de technicien* (BT), providing for entrance into a specific profession; or the *baccalauréat de technicien* (BTN), leading to further technical education. The large majority choose the general education option, in accordance with the widespread French belief that general education provides the best possibility for social and occupational success.

The French attitude toward vocational education at the secondary school level has been marked by ambivalence. While creating a variety of vocational schools in the course of the twentieth century, the French continue to recognize general education as the path of greatest prestige. In part, this reflects French egalitarianism derivative from the eighteenth century. The latent support for comprehensive education was expressed in the reforms of 1975, which all but abolished vocational education at the lower secondary level. The choice of students is already undermining specialized vocational education at the upper secondary level. France is beginning to look more like the United States. The British, on the other hand, have continued to resist the expansion of general education at the upper secondary level.

United Kingdom

The British system of vocational education was formed in the late nineteenth century, when a high-level report was commissioned to respond to fears that its vocational education system had deteriorated. The report recommended two parallel efforts: one focusing on practical training of prospective skilled workers and the other on their general education. Business firms were to organize the first, and educational establishments were to organize the second. Management and labor agreed to revive the atrophying apprenticeship programs, which were to be governed by collective agreements. Practical training was to last five years and end with recognition as a skilled craftsman and union member.

First efforts were made to include workers in general education, but later the emphasis was on creating technical colleges. In contrast to colleges in the United States, which admit graduates of upper secondary schools, the British colleges substitute for upper secondary education. While initially apprenticeships and technical colleges were run independently, in 1944 at attempt was made to encourage day release so that apprentices could attend the technical colleges. In 1947–48 less than 200,000 young people between the ages of 15 and 20 attended day schools, but by 1962–63 the number had risen to 445,000. And the number continues to rise. While the technical colleges enrollments have been increasing, they still represent a relatively small portion of the graduates of lower secondary schools. The general upper secondary schools have also remained small, catering to those who go on to higher education.

As late as 1974 over half of those leaving lower secondary school entered the labor force at age 15 or 16. Only 20 percent entered upper secondary school. However, as youth unemployment has remained high in the period since the mid–1970s, the pressures to expand educational opportunities have increased. In the short period from 1974 to 1977 the percentage of young people entering full-time general or vocational education doubled to 42 percent.

Explaining the European Experience

Rising youth unemployment, which was recognized in the United States during the 1960s and became even more noticeable during the 1970s, did not surface in Europe until the aftermath of the 1973–74 recession. The American model of broad-based upper secondary education has appeared attractive in a world in which the nature of jobs and work is constantly changing. Doesn't such a world require broad education, which makes the individual adaptable to changing job requirements?

As the French, British, and Scandinavian countries have attempted to respond to the needs of youth during the 1970s, they have expanded the upper secondary school. Of course there is another powerful imperative favoring this approach. A system of extended vocational education provides a powerful labor supply effect in times of a lessened demand for labor. As students are absorbed by the school system instead of the work place, especially in the years that education is extended, they relieve the pressures on the labor market. In the long term, the extension of schooling reduces the years during which individuals are available in the labor market. The result has been recognized by the trade unions in the United States, England, Sweden, and France, all of whom invariably favor such an extension.

While the extension of the upper secondary school has been almost universal, the separate vocational school has had varying support. Japan has virtually ignored it, Sweden has incorporated it into the comprehensive school, and France has supported it with a distinct ambivalence. It has fared better in the United Kingdom. Germany continues to maintain and increase its vocational schools, but also relies upon the *Duales System.*

In the middle of the nineteenth century, while in other European countries the apprenticeship system was atrophying, reforms in Germany were made to protect apprentices and enforce school attendance. In 1897 the *Duales System* was established, including practical and theoretical training. The most common approach was practical training in the company supplemented by attendance at an educational facility. Other alternatives included training and education in a workshop school or an apprenticeship school run by the firm or combined training and education in an independent vocational school referred to as *Berufsfachschule*, which was the least popular. As late as 1960 only 140,000 trainees attended vocational school, while some 1,189,225 apprenticeship contracts were registered.

Education is compulsory for all those below the age of 18, including apprentices. A formal system was established requiring apprentices to spend eight hours per week in a vocational school for a period of three years. By statute in 1937 a distinction was made among three types of vocational schools: *Berufschulen*, which provide general vocational education for apprentices and others; *Berufsfachschulen*, which provide both education and classroom training; and *Fachschulen*, which are advanced training schools for technicians. The *Duales System* of course is quite distinctive and emphasizes on-the-job training rather than in-school education. Its operation and future potential will be described in Chapter 5.

THE FUTURE OF SCHOOL-BASED VOCATIONAL EDUCATION

American vocational education both expressed the initial interests of the business and labor groups and reinforced those interests through the development of a system that prolonged schooling and externalized responsibility for skill training. The system encouraged the development of a highly mobile labor force, where individuals moved freely among jobs and firms invested minimally in training.

Vocational education was a pathbreaking initiative in 1917 and reinforced the American commitment to universal upper secondary education. The American system became a model for the rest of the world, yet its shortcomings have become increasingly apparent. The connection between the world of work and the educational system that vocational education was supposed to reinforce, has weakened.

In the early 1960s James Conant called attention to a slum section in a large city in which 59 percent of the males between 16 and 21 were out of school and unemployed.[8] Of the boys who graduated from high school, 48 percent were unemployed, as opposed to 63 percent of those who left school. Wondering whether this state of affairs provided much incentive to complete high school, Conant found it necessary to propound the "heretical" view that the educational experiences of youth in an urbanized, industrialized free society needed to fit their subsequent employment.

American vocational education, in fact, has never successfully provided job-specific training. The difficulties of arranging training for a group of students who will be entering different work places and the difficulty of ensuring that the teachers have the specific training appropriate to these work situations is formidable. Some inventive approaches have been developed, which usually require a second-stage training program on company facilities. A variation of this approach is to require part of the student's training to involve a work placement. Vocational education may also have difficulty in instilling the skills associated with work socialization: knowing how to deal with others on the job, accepting supervision and guidance, and understanding and conforming to the norms of the work place.

Vocational education has also suffered from the rapid development of new careers within business and slowness in adaptation. Because the vocational education system remains separated from the work situation and the teachers often do not have opportunities to update their own skills, the training can easily become obsolete. This problem of adaptation is further exacerbated by the costs of providing updated training facilities. As new machinery is used, the training facilities often become obsolete, but the school systems may not be able to afford the costs of replacing these materials. Sometimes ad hoc arrangements are made by local employers to provide such equipment, but unless they are directly benefiting from a flow of trained students, they have little incentive to provide costly equipment.

The other major shortcoming of the American system of universal education has been its inability to deal effectively with school leavers. As upper secondary school became nearly universal for those up to the age of 18, the rates of drop-out and absence from secondary schools have increased.

Formerly, of course, those students who rebelled against secondary school education for whatever reasons were part of the group of school leavers who could find work in a variety of career options. But as the job market has tightened and as fewer students have left school, the career options for these youth have nearly disappeared. While this has broadened the interest in continuing school, it has also created a greater dilemma for those who leave school. It hardly seems a sensible suggestion to try to force them back to school. Yet this is exactly what most countries are trying to do in the face of tight labor markets.

School leavers can also be viewed as rebels against their dependent student status. School attending involves acceptance of subordination to parents and teachers. It means a lack of financial resources and submission to the discipline of the classroom, which is often more pervasive than that of the work place. For this reason, training programs that remove some of the constraints of the school setting and provide financial resources may directly address some of the needs of school leavers. In fact, what is ironical about the continual extension of schooling in the 1960s and 1970s and its associated dependent status is that youth today may be better prepared to enter the adult world than in earlier times. Yet the extension of schooling for many of these youth who are ready to assume adulthood means deferring the fulfillment of this basic need. The reimposition of additional schooling or even training under these circumstances is counterproductive. In the absence of jobs or training places, the alternatives are limited.

In recent years there have been other indications the generalist approach of American secondary education is not adequately preparing youth for the world of work. The career education movement has done much to reemphasize the need to include vocational preparation throughout school. The need to provide skill training for those entering the labor force is also critical.

Another dimension of this movement is the emphasis on the importance of work experience, by bringing the world of work into the classroom and by taking the students directly into the world of work. High schools throughout the country have developed work experience programs in conjunction with local businesses. As larger numbers of American youth have deferred entrance into work to attend upper secondary school, the numbers first entering the work force through temporary jobs have increased. Although a substantial portion of this involvement involves part-time work that neither requires nor imparts formalized training, the experiences can be quite helpful in developing better work attitudes and interpersonal skills. Ordinarily these jobs contribute minimally to occupational skills.

Some of these part-time positions provide skill training as well. Co-operative education programs to place students in part-time jobs through the intervention of the school system sometimes develop such positions. When these jobs are properly supervised and chosen, they may make a marked contribution to the student's understanding of the world of work and even contribute directly to occupational skills development. Where cooperative education programs integrate vocational education with on-the-job training (OJT), they provide a particularly valuable connection for the young. Often in these situations, an employment relation will develop after graduation.

In building upon the current American educational system, it is the strengths of the broad-based comprehensive education that need to be stressed, including the integration of vocational preparation into the comprehensive high school curriculum. The report of the Advisory Council on Vocational Education, *The Bridge Between Man and His Work*, which was prepared for Congress as it contemplated the amendments to the Vocational Education Act of 1968, stressed the need for an integrated approach to vocational education, which is still relevant today.

It is no longer possible to compartmentalize education into general, academic, and vocational components. Education is a crucial element in preparation for a successful working career at any level. . . . The educational skills of spoken and written communication, computation, analytic techniques, knowledge of society and one's role in it, and skill in human relations are as vital as the skills of particular occupations. On the other hand, employability skills are equally essential to education. . . .

Vocational education is not a separate discipline, but it is a basic objective of all education and must be a basic element of each person's education. . . . Skill development can be accomplished through work experience or through education in the school's shops and laboratories. The key is to build a better means of integrating academic education, skill training, and work experience.[9]

The future of American vocational education, then, rests on both integrating skill training into a comprehensive secondary education and ensuring that preparation for the world of work is a pervasive concern of education.

In a world of developing and changing technology, skills in written and oral expression, and interpersonal relations, as well as analytic abilities become critical. These are the skills that the comprehensive high school is well equipped to teach. Time and again business executives emphasize the importance of these basic skills in making for successful integration into the work force. They often express the view that they prefer to teach specific occupational skills themselves.

Vocational education works best when the ties between local companies and local education authorities are close and cooperative. But these developments seem to depend on happenstance and individual personality rather than being built into the system. Too often the division of responsibilities between the companies and the schools results in business criticism of the quality and relevance of education and school criticism of business for not employing local youth.

Indeed, the most successful vocational education programs have been those that have combined classroom instruction with OJT within the firm. The need for close cooperation between the school and the employer in occupational training is clear. What is needed is a greater commitment on the part of the employers and a comprehensive system for involving them in this aspect of education.

In reviewing the development of vocational education in the United States, the guiding principle is clearly the integration of vocational education into the framework of general secondary education. In spite of the tendency to establish a special system of manual training schools and the institutionalization of special schools and departments encouraged by the federal funding mechanism, the tendency today is to deemphasize the separateness of vocational education.

The comprehensive view of vocational education points to the need for every secondary school graduate to understand the world of work. Furthermore, the graduate must develop skills that will facilitate a successful career. Within that framework it must be recognized that the need for specific skills will be greater for those students not continuing on immediately to higher education. There is no reason for those who have definitely decided not to attend higher education not to devote more time to obtaining job skills. It is questionable whether placing such students in special vocational schools is necessary. The tendency today is to deemphasize the advantages of special schools. Perhaps their greatest value is in imparting specialized skills over short periods of time just prior to job market entry.

This approach to vocational education is clearly being followed by Sweden and Japan. Both countries have very large and growing proportions of their students attending secondary school until age 17 or 18 and then going on to university. France has moved to comprehensive lower secondary education and, if the analysis above is correct, will be moving toward such a system at the upper secondary school. Germany, with its distinctive dual system, still emphasizes apprenticeships from ages 15 to 18. Yet the numbers completing secondary school and going on to university are increasing. The United Kingdom has also seen the expansion of students in general secondary education as well as the expansions of the system of colleges beyond the lower secondary school. These colleges maintain a decidedly specialized emphasis, leaving the United Kingdom perhaps the farthest from the creation of a universal, comprehensive secondary school system up to the age of 18.

The powerful draw of the American system and its progress in bringing skill training within a comprehensive framework notwithstanding, the need to address its shortcomings should not be forgotten. It has not provided adequate training in specific job skills, and it has not adequately addressed the needs of those students who do not complete full-time secondary education and are rejected by the system. These continuing problems suggest that comprehensive school-based education at the upper secondary school level is not sufficient by itself.

NOTES

1. Roger Gregoire, *Vocational Education* (Paris: Organization for Economic Cooperation and Development, 1967), p. 32.

2. August C. Bolino, *Career Education* (New York: Praeger, 1973).

3. See, for example, Marvin Lazerson and W. Norton Grubb, eds., *American Education and Vocationalism* (New York: Teachers College, 1974).

4. See, for example, Joel Spring, "The American High School and the Development of Social Character," in Walter Feinberg and Henry Rosenmount, Jr., eds., *Work, Technology, and Education* (Urbana: University of Illinois Press, 1975).

5. David B. Tyack, ed., *Turning Points in American Educational History* (New York: Wiley, 1967), p. 360.

6. *Primary and Secondary Education in Sweden* (Stockholm: Swedish Institute, 1981); Nordic Council of Ministers, *Youth Guarantee: Theory or Reality* (Secretariat of the Nordic Council of Ministers, June 1981). See also personal interviews listed in appendix.

7. *Comparative Study of the Financial, Legislative and Regulatory Structure of Vocational Training Systems* (Berlin: European Centre for the Development of Vocational Training [CEDEFOP], 1980). See also personal interviews listed in appendix.

8. James B. Conant, *Slums and Suburbs* (New York: McGraw-Hill, 1961), p. 33.

9. The Advisory Council on Vocational Education, *Vocational Education: The Bridge Between Man and His Work* (Washington, D.C.: Government Printing Office, 1968).

CHAPTER 3

Why CETA Failed

A CONFUSION OF PURPOSE

The limitations of vocational education, particularly its inability to deal with unemployed school leavers, led to an alternative system of job training under the U.S. Department of Labor. This system was begun by the Manpower Development and Training Act of 1962 (MDTA) and greatly expanded by other Great Society programs during the 1960s. In 1973 MDTA was replaced by the Comprehensive Employment and Training Act (CETA), which was perhaps the most controversial social legislation of the 1970s. Between 1974 and 1981 it cost over $52 billion. Its predecessor MDTA had cost $10 billion between 1967 and 1973. In 1977 alone more than $12 billion was expended to provide support for more than 4.5 million individuals.

In truth CETA represented only a portion of the American commitment to employment and training assistance. During 1977 more than $5 billion was appropriated under the Vocational Education Act; the Armed Forces spent between $9 billion and $10 billion on vocational training; and the private sector spent $30–40 billion for both classroom and OJT training. The other smaller programs included HEW's Work Incentive Program (WIN) funded at $245 million; vocational education through the Social and Rehabilitation Services at $79 million; adult education at $79 million; and training in correctional institutions at $14 million. The Justice, Transportation, and Treasury departments each provided at least $10 million a year in funds for vocational training, while other civilian training programs in the federal government enrolled an additional 515,000 individuals. Not to be forgotten were the more than 200,000 persons enrolled in junior colleges and other postsecondary occupational programs in the public sector. Private sector proprietary schools enrolled about 1.8 million, while apprenticeship programs enrolled about 255,000 workers. Yet CETA, because of its visibility, assumed a peculiar symbolism in American politics. Newly elected President Reagan moved swiftly to curtail the program in 1980.

CETA meant different things to different people, but it is probably fair to say that it was perceived as a failure by the great majority of the American public. Despite its promise to train and employ millions of workers, it was perceived as a make-work program that left its beneficiaries without employment and more frustrated than ever. If this global judgment was partially true, it also fails to account for CETA's successes.

CETA's roots can be traced to the period following World War II, when pressures developed for a national policy to avoid a repetition of the unemployment of the 1930s.[1] Many feared that the rapid demobilization in the postwar period would immediately lead to a resumption of unemployment. The raising of the unemployment issue during the presidential campaign of 1944 and the agreement of candidates Roosevelt and Dewey about the need for action led to the adoption of the Employment Act of 1946. While the Employment Act of 1946 set the admirable goal of full employment, it did little to move the country toward a realistic manpower policy. The World War II GI Bill of Rights had a far greater impact on people's lives. The GI Bill spent some $14.5 billion on training benefits and led to an additional $4.5 billion for training post–World War II veterans. It also had a powerful legitimizing impact on later national efforts to provide job training assistance.

In the 1950s, efforts at a national manpower policy lagged because employment was generally high. During the 1960 presidential election campaign rising unemployment, from 5.1 percent in May to 6.2 percent in November, gave impetus to Senator Paul Douglas's efforts to enact the Areas Redevelopment Act of 1961. That economic development measure provided low interest loans and grants for community facilities to stimulate economic development and job creation in depressed areas. A small portion of the act, providing $14.5 million for job training in the first year, became the model for the Manpower Development and Training Act (MDTA) of 1962.

Support for a broader training bill, extending beyond depressed areas, began developing in Congress while the Areas Redevelopment Act was awaiting executive approval. This new legislation became the province of the new Senate Subcommittee on Employment and Manpower, chaired by Senator Joseph Clark of Pennsylvania. The Clark proposal called for the addition of a new category to the Smith-Hughes Act of 1917 to provide federal grants in aid for training those who were unemployed as a result of "structural changes." It also extended training allowances to those ineligible for unemployment compensation.

Labor Department Secretary Arthur Goldberg, acting under assignment from President Kennedy, took the administration lead and proposed an alternative bill, which placed the Secretary of Labor in control and authorized full federal financing rather than matching grants. Both state vocational facilities and on-the-job training (OJT) were to be used. The bill that passed, in an amended form, became the Manpower Development and Training Act.

MDTA attracted widespread, bipartisan support, in part because of its ability to encompass contradictory aspirations and views of the American economy. For Senator Joseph Clark, its chief Senate sponsor, it was an opportunity to train residents of depressed communities for new jobs, mirroring a program in Pennsylvania with which he was familiar. For Congressman Elmer Holland, the chief House sponsor, it was a defense against the automation that he saw as a threat to his own constituents working in Pennsylvania steel mills. To some like William McChesney Martin, chairman of the Federal Reserve Board, and Arthur Burns, future chairman of the Federal Reserve Board, it was a reaffirmation of their belief that no shortage of jobs existed for individuals possessing the proper skills.

Underlying these disagreements was the question of the extent to which unemployment could be attributed to technological and structural changes in the American economy, versus the belief that unemployment reflected the lack of growth in an increasingly productive economy facing an expanding labor force. This confusion of purpose and underlying disagreement about the causes of unemployment were to hound MDTA and its successor CETA and are still not resolved.

THE EVOLUTION OF MDTA

The number of specific programs that came within the employment and training umbrella quickly proliferated. Two such programs established by the Economic Opportunity Act of 1964 (EOA) were the Neighborhood Youth Corps (NYC) and the Job Corps. NYC offered subsidized work experience in public and private agencies to those in school between the ages of 14 and 21. In addition the NYC summer program provided nine weeks of part-time work in the summer. Originally work experience was also provided for those out of school, but by 1980 they were receiving skills training and supportive services. The Job Corps was an intensive residential program for disadvantaged youth that provided subsistence jobs along with skills training and basic literacy and numeracy instruction. The vocational fields include clerical, culinary arts, construction, automotive mechanics, and health.

MDTA emphasized locally based programs, administered by two existing public agencies: the public schools and the Employment Service

(ES). The ES was able to identify eligible people and suitable occupational goals, while the schools could provide skills training. Competing with programs lodged in the schools (the institutional component of MDTA), was on-the-job training (OJT), a program to reimburse local employers for the costs of training. The failure of these programs to provide the number of training places anticipated is discussed fully in the next chapter.

In subsequent years, as the War on Poverty gained prominence, MDTA programs became oriented toward a disadvantaged clientele. By 1966, the DOL had declared the objective of spending at least 65 percent of its monies for training the disadvantaged. In 1968, reinforcing this targeting approach, the disadvantaged were specifically defined as those who were both poor and without satisfactory employment plus (1) under 21 or over 44 years of age; (2) without a high school degree; (3) a member of a minority group; or (4) physically or mentally handicapped. MDTA became perceived as a program to help the poor and the minorities. This perception had a chilling effect on the OJT program, which depended upon private employers to provide training sites. CETA was perceived by private employers as a social welfare program rather than a program in support of their operations, so that while large corporations might feel compelled to participate at least once, the long-term viability of the program was undermined. Indeed, as the focus on the disadvantaged was emphasized, the number of OJT placements diminished.

By the late 1960s a dozen separate categorical programs, each with its own appropriation account, had come within the purview of the DOL's Manpower Administration. Office of Economic Opportunity (OEO) funds were granted directly to community action agencies, schools, voluntary agencies, and businesses. A major alternative called skill centers was developed jointly by OEO and DOL under the institutional aid component. These skill centers were independent of the local school systems, creating a separate group of independent contractors.

After a decade of operation, by 1973, the programs coming under MDTA had established a sizable number of places for youth. NYC and the Job Corps were exclusively for youth. Youth also represented a substantial proportion of those in institutional training and a sizable proportion of those served by the Public Employment Program (PEP). Only a small percentage of OJT slots went to those aged 16 to 19. Table 3.1 indicates the number of places in each category.

As program sponsors and program monitors proliferated, problems in coordination arose. One response was the Concentrated Employment Program (CEP), modeled after a Chicago program known as Jobs Now. CEP called for the establishment of comprehensive service cen-

Table 3.1
Numbers of Youth Served, 1963–1973

Program	Number
MDTA Institutional	565,600
Neighborhood Youth Corps	
In-school	1,130,600
Out-of-school	771,300
Summer	3,048,200
Total	4,950,100
Job Corps	184,800
Public Employment Program	179,000

Source: Employment and Training Report of the President (Washington, D.C.: Government Printing Office, 1980), p. 82.

ters in poverty areas that could perform outreach and intake, work orientation, referral to job training or job placement, and supportive services including basic education and health services.

Another effort to achieve coordination was the Cooperative Area Manpower Planning System (CAMPS), which sought to establish coordinating committees at the area, state, regional, and national levels. But the problems of coordination that were set loose by the proliferation of categorical programs finally led to the adoption of the Comprehensive Employment and Training Act of 1973 (CETA).

Even before CETA was enacted, though, the rising unemployment rate led to a separate initiative that was to have a profound impact on the future of CETA. This new departure was the Emergency Employment Act of 1971, which provided $2.25 billion for a program of public sector jobs known as the Public Employment Program (PEP). This program soon came to dominate CETA and strongly influence the debate about employment and training policy.

HERE COMES CETA

CETA represented a major shift from a Washington-run categorical program to a locally administered program funded through objective formulae. It was one of the Nixon administrations heralded special revenue-sharing measures.[2] The federal government provided funds, and programs were administered by local prime sponsors. Small areas that could not support their own prime sponsor would be administered by the state functioning itself as a prime sponsor. While the Department of Labor maintained final authority, administrative decisions were concentrated at the prime sponsor level.

Most of the previously developed services were included in Title I of CETA, providing for a nationwide program of training, employment, and counseling. Decisions about which projects to fund in a specific locality were up to the prime sponsors, guided by local advisory boards. The PEP program created by the Emergency Employment Act of 1971 was incorporated in Title II, which became known as Public Service Employment (PSE). In the original legislation, areas with a 6.5 percent or higher unemployment rate for three consecutive months were eligible for special funding of public service jobs. Title III created a nationally sponsored and supervised training, employment, and job placement program for groups with particular labor market disadvantages. The highly successful Job Corps was funded through Title IV. Title V created a National Commission for Manpower Policy, an advisory group to help with long-range planning.

While the more salient issue during the adoption of CETA was decentralization of authority, the incorporation of PEP was to have the more profound effect. The impact of Title II and subsequently Title VI, the countercyclical program of public jobs, was to shift the entire orientation of CETA. As the recession of 1974–1975 made jobs more difficult to find, the efforts to locate OJT places were curtailed. Instead, prime sponsors spent their time and efforts mounting, funding, and monitoring public service employment programs.

Another development in CETA was the expansion of Title IV to include several additional youth related programs established by the Youth Employment Demonstration Projects Act of 1977 (YEDPA). YEDPA roughly doubled expenditures for youth programs. The major new departures were the Youth Incentive Entitlement Pilot Projects (YIEPP), designed to help economically disadvantaged youth complete high school; the Youth Employment and Training Programs (YETP), which sought to enhance the job prospects and career preparation of low-income youth between the ages of 14 and 21; and some special demonstration projects funded through discretionary funds provided to the secretary of labor. In addition, the Summer Youth Employment Program and the Job Corps were expanded, and two new programs were created: the Youth Community Conservation and Improvement Projects and the Youth-Adult Conservation Corps.

In 1978 CETA was reauthorized and its titles were rearranged. Title I was reserved for general administrative provisions. Title II contained comprehensive services, including training, work experience, education, and other services, as parts A, B and C. Part D was public service employment. Title III authorized the Secretary of Labor to provide services to populations experiencing particular disadvantages in the labor market. Title IV included the various youth programs authorized by YEDPA. Title V continued the National Commission for Manpower

Policy, now renamed the National Commission for Employment Policy. A countercyclical program of public service jobs was authorized by Title VI. Title VII created demonstration projects to test the effectiveness of a variety of measures to increase the involvement of the private sector in CETA. Title VII provided funds to prime-sponsors to establish private industry councils (PICs) to facilitate the development of private sector projects.

During fiscal 1980 over 2 million persons were enrolled under CETA Titles IIB, C, and D and Title VI. Of the 2 million approximately 800,000 were below the age of 22. An additional half-million individuals were enrolled in youth programs under Title IV.

While the administration of the CETA programs improved over time, its impact was questionable. As unemployment remained high, the link between training and job placements lagged. When job placements were obtained, for example in fast food chains, the charge was made that the funds were being used to support cheap labor rather than to obtain training for career positions.

While the public was willing to fund public sector jobs for a limited duration, eventually the limits of this approach became apparent. Public sector jobs did not lead to private sector employment. Unless the programs were extended, their beneficiaries would be unemployed once more.

In 1982 the new Jobs Training Partnership Act (JTPA) replaced CETA. It eliminated the public sector jobs program and reduced funding in other areas but maintained such programs as the Job Corps, the Summer Youth Employment Program, and the private industry councils. With rising unemployment it remains a mystery, however, how these training programs will be any more successful in achieving placements than have CETA programs in the past.

LESSONS FROM CETA

What, then, have we learned from the CETA experience? What benefits have accrued to the individuals in the programs? Aside from benefits to individuals, has the society at large benefited? Posing this question from a human capital perspective, is the investment being made in increased skills bringing a reasonable return, given possible alternative uses of society's resources? Such an analysis requires data over a number of years (longitudinal data) and rigorous control procedures. The lifetime earnings of participants in training and employment programs must be compared to similar individuals lacking such program benefits. Then the return on the investment of society's resources must be compared to alternative possibilities, for example, in direct payments, general economic stimulus, or differently organized training programs. The effects of such programs on the labor market must be considered. Is the government merely paying to displace another equally competent individual? Are jobs being filled that would otherwise remain unoccupied or would be filled by less qualified personnel?

A major shortcoming of the evaluations of employment and training programs is the lack of longitudinal data. This results from the demands of day-to-day operations, which allow little time for record keeping, and from the difficulties of maintaining records and follow-ups on individuals once they have left a program. Such difficulties have long been associated with more traditional vocational education programs. In both areas the costs and difficulties of maintaining records are reinforced by the fears of program administrators that evaluations may show small effects at best. Why should they support evaluations that are not likely to strengthen their case for more institutional support? Such a phenomenon, of course, is not unique to training programs. Evaluation shyness exists in most operating organizations.

A rich literature has developed to interpret the successes and failures of MDTA and CETA and the myriad programs that came under their aegis.[3] Some programs were outstanding. Most everyone agrees that the Job Corps has been a great success and should be continued. Supported work projects for AFDC (Aid to Families with Dependent Children) mothers have also been successful. The Jobs Now private sector initiative launched in the early 1960s in Chicago is generally praised and was used as a model for other programs. Yet the substantive basis for praising CETA is not impressive.

The majority of MDTA and CETA evaluations used the simple before–after assessment, where an individual's annual earnings before receiving training are compared to earnings after completion of the program. These studies on the whole indicate a rise in income. Magnum and Walsh in their summary of the progress of MDTA, written in anticipation of the passage of CETA, argued that a substantial gain in earnings resulted from participation in MDTA.[4] Using all available records of terminees in the fiscal years 1971 and 1972, they found 15.5 percent and 14.6 percent gains in average hourly wages during fiscal 1971 for institutional and OJT enrollees, respectively. For fiscal 1972, gains of 8.7 percent for institutional and 6.3 percent for OJT enrollees were recorded. Magnum and Walsh then corrected for the average hourly earnings gains of all production workers (5.9 percent in 1971 and 4.1 percent in 1972) and concluded that MDTA was indeed effective. They then calculated earnings gains of $1,621 for institutional and $1,336 for OJT enrollees. A later policy statement by the National Council on Employment Policy cited some of the same studies relied upon by Magnum and Walsh and concluded that institutional training resulted in earnings increases from $1,100 to $1,900 and OJT resulted in slightly higher increases. Perry, Anderson, Rowan, and Northrup, in their analysis of employment and training programs, also found substantial earnings gains.

Each of these major commentators recognized the need for controlled experimentation and the lack of it in the employment and training field. Magnum and Walsh were able to cite only one major study using controls, selected retrospectively. The National Council on Employment Policy cited a number of studies using controls, but none are identified as true experimental designs. These studies indicated a tremendous variability in earnings gains over control groups. For example, earnings gains for nonwhite females ranged from $200 to $1,600, and for white males from $48 to $557. The use of such techniques as comparing actual earnings differentials to average changes in earnings of large populations, projecting earnings increases of single years over long periods of time, and selecting control groups retrospectively raises serious questions about the value of these findings. Doubts are reinforced by studies which show that even these earnings differentials drop off sharply after the first year.

An exception to this lack of rigor in evaluations of CETA programs is the recent evaluation of the Job Corps program by Mathematica Policy Research, which does use rigorous control procedures and has found demonstrable gains in income.[5] Admittedly, this program has been viewed as one of the most successful. So far the evaluation only extends to a period of two years after program completion, and the gains are modest. But they demonstrate that at least this CETA program does increase individual earnings while it reduces dependency and criminal behavior.

The perceived failure of CETA by the American public, then, is not contradicted by program evaluation statistics. The Job Corps evaluation is impressive, but it cannot be logically extended to other programs. In fact, its modest impacts would seem to cast doubt on the efficacy of other less highly regarded programs. It should be pointed out, however, that many CETA programs have been initiated during periods of economic recession and increasing competition in the labor market, when employers have been highly selective in hiring. As these programs focused more and more on the most disadvantaged, they were in fact focusing on those at the end of the job queue.

The paradox of CETA, then, is that when the labor market is strong individuals will be absorbed regardless of training. When the labor market is weak, participation in CETA may reinforce an individual's position at the end of the job queue. In this sense CETA was destined for the failure it attained. Was all the money down the drain then? In one sense, yes. In another sense, no.

CETA has provided training experience for millions of Americans who would otherwise have been unemployed. The value to these individuals in terms of self-esteem, individual growth, and success in these programs is immeasurable. Their addition to the productive capacity of government and private sector organizations was substantial. Without CETA, many would have been unemployed and unproductive. By providing them with a productive outlet as an alternative to unemployment, CETA was a success. But it was never sold to the American public on this basis. Indeed, if proposed on this basis it might never have been accepted.

The CETA experience also pointed up some failures of the existing American educational system and youth labor market. A large proportion of the CETA trainees were high school dropouts and high school graduates who could not find jobs. As these individuals completed CETA programs, their deferred introduction to the youth labor market took place. Most either could find no jobs or were hired into jobs they could have obtained without training. The youth labor market that did exist consisted of temporary jobs without a future. Something had happened to that great American dream of going into the world of opportunity, finding a place, working hard, and becoming successful.

Just as CETA was coming into effect, Europe was confronted by the recession of 1973–1974. The recession and its aftermath left the European countries with a growing unemployment problem, with youth unemployment the most serious of all. The CETA experience provided an important precedent in this area as each European country in its own way sought to cope with youth unemployment. Many of the mistakes of CETA were repeated in Europe. The lessons of social experimentation are learned slowly.

CETA'S EUROPEAN COUNTERPARTS

In one respect, the orientation of the European countries was initially different from that of the United States. While in the United States the CETA program had come to be viewed as a major effort to assist the disadvantaged obtain the skills they needed for success in the job market, the Europeans viewed their youth measures as a temporary expedient to assist young people caught in an economic recession. Only after the unemployment problem continued into the 1980s did the Europeans realize that their temporary measures had become semipermanent and that long-range solutions were necessary.

This short-term perspective is perhaps most clearly seen in France, which first enacted Projet 50,000, followed by a series of three successive national programs, Les Pactes Nationaux pour l'Emploi. Each time it was believed that these short-term measures once completed would not need to be reenacted.[6] In their report of May 1977, *Young People and*

Work, the Manpower Services Commission in the United Kingdom summarized the impact of their previous measures: "Every scheme has been introduced on a temporary basis. This has inhibited employers and others from making the provision they could make—and would like to make—if they could be sure that there was some commitment for at least two or three years ahead."[7] In Sweden, a program of public relief work that nearly eliminated unemployment among 16–18 year olds was deemphasized when it became obvious that it discouraged school attendance and longer-range solutions were necessary.[8]

But having recognized the problem of youth unemployment as a continuing one, each of the European countries has continued to innovate into the 1980s in an attempt to be more successful. All three seem on the verge of adopting a guarantee for youth between the ages of 16 and 18 of full-time schooling, full-time work, or a training experience.

France

Les Pactes Nationaux pour l'Emploi in France, were a series of measures aimed at encouraging firms to hire and train young people. Their total cost between 1977 and 1980 was $910 million francs. They included a broad spectrum of youth, including substantial numbers holding university and professional degrees, although approximately 20 percent of the males and 40 percent of the females had not obtained an upper secondary diploma. Some of the measures involved nothing more than monetary incentives to employers to hire young people. Three major programs developed that are of particular concern here: Stages en Centres de Formation, Contrats Emploi-Formation, and Stages Pratiques en Entreprises.

Stages en Centre de Formation included a range of state-financed training courses for those between the ages of 16 and 25, intended to provide entry into a profession. During the training, which could last up to 6 months, the trainee, depending upon age, would receive from 25 to 90 percent of the minimum wage. Contrats Emploi-Formation were employment contracts entered into between a person ages 17 to 25 and a private firm. The employer would pay the holder a salary and assume the cost of agreed-upon training. The government provided a subsidy to the employer and allowed for the waiver of social security taxes. Approximately 50 percent of those participating remained with the employers in regular positions after the subsidized contract was complete. Stages Pratique en Entreprises consisted of practical in-firm training courses of between 4 and 8 months' duration held in conjunction with a formal training course of at least 120 hours duration. The employer paid the trainee an allowance equal to 90 percent of the officially recognized minimum wage for those over 18. The state paid the

Table 3.2
Les Pactes Nationaux pour l'Emploi

	First Pacte 7/77/–2/78	Second Pacte 7/78–3/79	Third Pacte 7/79–6/80
Stages en Centres	68,652	55,915	46,227
Contrats Emploi	26,354	38,120	64,253
Stages Pratiques	145,679	20,332	55,303

Source: Ministère du travail et de la participation, Travail et Emploi (Paris: La Documentation Francaise, October, 1980, no. 6), p. 16.

cost of the trainee's stipend, but the firm paid the cost of training. Table 3.2 indicates the number of individuals in each category for the three separate pactes.

The French program demonstrated that employers can be persuaded to hire young people by providing government subsidies for support and training. However, the programs were relatively small so that their usefulness as overall approaches to the problem of youth unemployment are questionable.

While the current Socialist government seems more aware of the youth unemployment problem and its connection to other social manifestations of disenchanted youth, it has not yet translated that realization into a concrete program of large scope. The latest version of a national program, slated for fall 1982, was to involve a target of 100,000 places for 16 and 17 year olds. Stress is being laid upon changes in the system of education so that every young person leaves school with a professional qualification. The principle of alternance is being encouraged so that young people may work and return to school. While the ideal of a comprehensive program for 16–18 year olds has been inititated, concrete steps to such a program have yet to be realized. France avoided the large-scale mistakes of the United States but has not yet proposed a solution capable of dealing with its large-scale problems.

Sweden

Sweden is a small country whose youth unemployment problem has been small, closer to that of Germany and Japan than that of the United States, the United Kingdom, or France. Yet the depth of the concern for the problem is perhaps the highest, reflecting in part the social welfare orientation of the Swedish people and in part the difficulty of depersonalizing the problem in a small country. Sweden has most closely copied the U.S. approach to upper secondary education; 80 percent of 16 and 17 year olds attend the comprehensive secondary school.

It also was the only other country to embark upon a massive public sector employment program. The Swedish Work Relief Program, which involved 50,000 young people over a period of two years, dramatically reduced unemployment but was also quite expensive since the workers received market wages. In addition, it suffered the same difficulty of similar CETA programs, namely, the lack of a future for those completing the artificially created jobs. Under an act of Parliament in May 1980, the so-called Youth Bill, the program was terminated, and primary responsibility for 16 and 17 year olds was returned to school authorities. Efforts were made to expand school facilities to accommodate an ever larger proportion of the age cohort. In addition, a program of vocational introduction was begun, providing young people the equivalent of the educational allowance. While employers have supported the program, the trade unions have opposed the low level of compensation.

As a result, a new program has been developed with the cooperation of the employers and employees, to provide employment for 16 and 17 year olds of up to six months, subject to mutual agreement between the employer and the trade union. While no guarantee of continued employment is included, it is expected that the jobs will provide valuable developmental experiences for the young people. The company is required to pay the young workers 85 Swedish kroner per day and provide for social security payments. The government provides a grant of 75 Swedish kroner per day. The young people are to be referred by labor exchanges and schools, and where possible, training of one day a week under a teacher will be arranged.

United Kingdom

The United Kingdom was fortunate that when the crisis in youth unemployment hit it had already in place the Manpower Services Commission (MSC), which was responsible for industrial training throughout the country as well as industrywide training boards, which had been created by the Industrial Training Act of 1964. It adopted a variety of special measures designed to provide a quick fix for the "temporary" problem. In May 1977, in its publication *Young People and Work*, the MSC reviewed its progress to date and proposed a comprehensive plan for the future. Its program included a variety of training programs and job creation and subsidy programs. Total expenditures for fiscal 1976–77 were 106 million pounds. Over 117,000 individuals were included in the programs: Direct training, under the Training Services Administration (TSA); Work Experience; and Incentive Training Grants.

The largest program initially was the Incentive Training Grants Program, providing funding to industrial training boards to provide training and employment. A high proportion of trainees were successful and placed with employers upon completion of the initial training. This program has remained in effect, recently renamed the Training for Skills Program. The smallest program for 1976–77, including only 8,000 places, was the Work Experience Program (WEP). WEP provided practical experience in a range of trades for unemployed young people and was doubled to 15,000 for 1977–78. By 1981–82 it accounted for 242,000 placements, becoming the centerpiece of the youth training effort.

The continuing rise in youth unemployment led to expanded and reorganized programs. By 1981 three major programs emerged: the Youth Opportunities Program (YOP); Training for Skills Program (TSP); and Unified Vocational Preparation Program (UVP). The Training for Skills Program is described above. UVP is designed to cater to 16–19 year olds who enter jobs with little or no training. Begun on an experimental basis, it is currently projected for 18,000 enrollees in 1982–83, 30,000 by 1983–84, and 50,000 by 1984–85. UVP aims to improve the skills, attitudes, and knowledge of trainees. UVP courses are designed for specific industry sectors and average 60 days spread over a six-month period. The government pays for college fees, incentive grants to employers of four pounds per trainee day, any residential charge, and certain promotion and development charges.

The Youth Opportunities Program (YOP) accounts for all the remaining placements, which focus on courses designed to prepare young people to work and different kinds of work experience. These emphases are covered by six specific schemes: (1) Work Experience on Employer's Premises (WEEP), placing trainees directly with an employer; (2) Community Service (CS), wherein groups work on specific projects to aid the community; (3) Project Based Work Experience (PBWE), providing new services to the community; (4) Training Workshops (TW), which produce goods as well as provide training; (5) Work Introduction Courses (WIC), aimed to help low achievers acquire basic work, communication, and numeracy skills; and (6) Short Training Courses (STC), lasting for 13 weeks to lead to semiskilled jobs.

In a follow up survey of these YOP programs it was found that nearly 50 percent of the participants found jobs when they left the scheme, while nearly 40 percent were unemployed. Six months after the scheme, 60 percent were employed, while 20 percent remained unemployed, another 15 percent having reentered YOP. In spite of the fact that no effort was made to encourage employers to hire those completing WEEP, 32 percent were employed by their WEEP employer, while 23 percent found other jobs.

In May 1981 the Manpower Services Commission (MSC) presented *A New Training Initiative*, which projected an expansion of the Youth Opportunities Program to provide 440,000 places in 1981–82, working toward the point where every 16 and 17 year old who is not in education or a job will have an opportunity for a training experience. It also planned a sixfold increase in the experimental Unified Vocational Preparation (UVP) program. The plans of this document became formalized in *A New Training Initiative, An Agenda for Action* of December 1981, which in addition called for the active involvement of the employers and the trade unions. The *Youth Task Group Report* was the result of this collaboration among the MSC, the Confederation of British Industries (CBI), the Trades Union Congress (TUC), the local educational authorities, and other parties. The result was similar to that already suggested, but with slight changes, including a larger stipend for those participating and the specific commitment to provide training places for all 16 year olds and those unemployed 17 year olds, estimated at a total of 460,000 places. Additional emphasis is placed on improving the quality of training programs.

While it is too early to forecast success for the British scheme, it is instructive to note its differences from CETA. Like CETA it began as a program for disadvantaged youth, but as it expanded to youth generally it became an all-inclusive program. Unlike CETA it strictly limited the public sector job component to a manageable program of community service, which is often administered by nonprofit organizations. The British have avoided large-scale training programs outside the work place, where contractors develop a vested interest in continuing training programs regardless of their success.

While expanding the technical colleges, so far the British have resisted massive extension of upper secondary education as has occurred in the United States, Sweden, and Japan and to a lesser extent in Germany and France. If the new program is successful and the close cooperation of the employers and unions is encouraging, it could develop into a formidable system of OJT, similar to those in Germany and Japan. Since both the German and Japanese systems focus on in-firm training, they will be considered separately in Chapter 5.

TOWARD MORE REALISTIC EXPECTATIONS

Despite the benefits of upper secondary education, significant numbers of persons between the ages of 16 and 19 are not continuing their full-time studies. Even those who graduate from upper secondary school need help in making the transition to the world of work. These facts have been recognized by the CETA and other youth employment measures in this country and abroad.

All of these youth-oriented employment programs point up the need to deal with a growing number of secondary school dropouts and graduates who are having great difficulty in entering the job market. Handicapped by their position at the end of the job queue and the deteriorating position of youth in a service-oriented economy, those youth who most need guidance are least able to obtain it. Rather than getting extra assistance in finding career employment, these youth, who are already labeled failures because of their inability to continue on in the educational system, go from temporary job to temporary job without hope of permanent employment and without an opportunity to obtain job skills.

The varied youth training programs in the United States and abroad have proven that these youth are interested in improving their skills and will respond to the opportunities for real training and jobs. Many CETA programs provided a good environment and demonstrated that high-quality training programs could be mounted, but they were not particularly successful in leading these youth to career positions. What are needed are programs that can provide them entry into the world of work. It should be clear that a national training program cannot create a booming economy, nor can it reverse the position on the job queue of young workers, particularly if they are labeled disadvantaged. But perhaps it is time to admit that an approach focusing on the disadvantaged is doomed to failure in the face of an overriding need to reshape the system for effectuating the transition of 16–19 year olds into the world of work. Rather than building a broad consensus, it promotes division by attempting the impossible task of reversing the job market, by making the least desirable the most desirable. We need to create a viable system that works for all youth. By concentrating on those who have the hardest time, we emphasize the wrong approach at the wrong time. The need is for a system that provides places to the young in a systematic way and allows the private sector to pursue its basic and legitimate need for trained personnel.

Time and again administrators have recognized the critical importance of involving private sector employers through OJT programs. The French have emphasized private sector placements throughout the three Pactes Nationaux. In the first Pacte of over 500,000 places, only 70,000 involved training outside of a job situation. In the third Pacte of 390,000 places, less than 50,000 involved training without a job placement. The British WEEP program, involving placements in real work situations, has dwarfed their other programs and is currently being upgraded to provide more training places of higher quality. The Swedes, although emphasizing education, have also recently developed a program to place young workers for up to six months in OJT. And the Americans, though frustrated by a series of setbacks, have continually sought to secure OJT placements. Even today renewed efforts are being made following enactment of the Jobs Training Partnership Act of 1982 to develop greater support for OJT through the private industry councils (PICs). It is the Germans and Japanese, however, who have most fully grasped the potential of OJT for young workers and developed their entire systems of vocational education around this approach. OJT as a program and a philosophy is critical to an understanding of how training programs can help the young worker. More than any other approach it is successful in providing training placements with a future.

NOTES

1. On the development of the Manpower Development and Training Act of 1962, *see* G. L. Mangum, *MDTA, Foundations of Federal Manpower Policy* (Baltimore: Johns Hopkins University Press, 1968).

2. On the early developments in CETA, *see* William Mirengoff and Lester Rindler, *CETA: Manpower Programs Under Local Control* (Washington, D.C.: National Academy of Sciences, 1978).

3. For an expansion of this perspective, *see* David Bresnick, "CETA's Challenge to the Evaluation of Vocational Education," in *The Handbook of Vocational Education Evaluation*, ed. Carol Tittle and Theodore Abramson (Beverly Hills, Calif.: Sage, 1979).

4. G. L. Mangum and J. Walsh, *A Decade of Manpower Development and Training Programs* (Salt Lake City: Olympus, 1973).

5. Mathematica Policy Research, *Evaluation of the Economic Impact of the Job Corps Program, Third Follow-up Report* (Princeton, N.J.: Mathematica Policy Research, 1982).

6. F. Pate et al., "Les Pactes Nationaux pour l'Emploi des Jeunes," *Travail et emploi*, no. 6 (1980): 15–62.

7. Manpower Services Commission, *Young People and Work* (London: MSC, May 1977). Other relevant publications of the Manpower Services Commission include: *A New Training Initiative* (London: MSC, May 1981), and *Youth Task Group Report* (London: MSC, April 1982).

8. *See*, generally, Birgitta Magnusson, *What Is Being Done in Sweden for Unemployed 16 and 17 Year Olds?* (Stockholm: Swedish Institute, September 1981).

CHAPTER 4

OJT Is Hard to Legislate

AMERICAN BUSINESS EFFORTS TO TRAIN THE YOUNG

Although the Smith-Hughes Act committed the United States to vocational education in schools, it of course did not eliminate the need for companies to concern themselves with the training of new employees. Even if skill training in the schools closely followed company requirements, the need would always remain for orienting the new worker to specific company procedures and practices. In fact, the vocational schools never took over skill training to the extent that companies could avoid their own programs. Depending upon the available labor supply and their individual needs, businesses developed training programs involving on-the-job training (OJT) instruction as well as classroom training.

Most of the training of new employees occurs on the job without prior planning. As companies become more sophisticated in their approach to training, however, more formal programs are developed. Some companies, such as Kodak Park, the largest manufacturing division of Kodak Company, have large and sophisticated training departments.[1] This group has created apprenticeship programs in 16 skills, ranging from carpenter to glass blower. Each apprenticeship combines 480 classroom hours with OJT over a three-year period.

Training on the job may follow prescribed sequences and employ a variety of teaching aids. New employees may be given written orientation materials in the form of manuals and programmed instruction. While formal courses have been designed in some instances, there is a tendency toward greater reliance on OJT and "hands on" experience. Overall, 30 percent of the companies in one survey reported involving new employees in courses.

The most highly developed programs of initial training are probably the apprenticeship programs, both those officially registered and funded through the Bureau of Apprenticeship Training of the U.S. Department of Labor in the United States and those run by companies on their own.[2] During industrialization in the United States, as in Europe, apprenticeships became less prevalent. By the turn of the century the number of apprentices began increasing, although it fell once again during the Depression. The apprenticeship had developed out of the medieval craft system and was strongly backed by the craft unions. They saw it as a way of avoiding the evils of child labor while regulating the supply of labor that might come into competition with their journeyman membership. The numbers increased considerably after World War II, then decreased, and have recently been on the rise. The number of registered apprentices, 269,000, in 1970, however, represents a small portion of the total school-leaving population. Apprentices are concentrated in the building trades, metalworking, and printing industries. In an effort to avoid the restrictions of the Bureau of Apprenticeship Training, many companies have instituted their own apprenticeship training, but the exact numbers are unknown.

In recent years the need for more training on the job has led to a renewed interest in apprenticeship. However, because of many restrictions, it seems unlikely that business and labor will agree on its further expansion. A similar tendency has already been noted in Sweden and the United Kingdom.

A series of efforts has been made to achieve greater exposure for the world of business in the school system. A recent survey reported that over 80 percent of all firms have some program of student work experience. Other programs involve teaching or counseling students, student tours and visits, and providing materials and programs for teachers. But the trend toward work experience, including cooperative education, work-study, part-time and temporary jobs, and special summer programs promises to have a major impact on the role of business in the educational process.

In fact, the business community, or at least certain segments, seem to recognize the usefulness of increasing the work experience of youth. Specialized programs leading from vocational skills training in high schools to OJT programs in companies represent inventive and productive approaches to helping young people make the transition from school to work while maximizing the impact of public and private resources.

A recent survey of companies employing over 250 employees has estimated that approximately 400,000 students annually receive work experience, somewhat less than half at the secondary level. This number represented a ratio of about 2 students for every 100 full-time employees. Slightly less than half of the students are at the secondary school level, representing 2.7 percent of all working-age eleventh- and twelfth-grade students. The majority of these are involved in cooperative education programs.

Cooperative education programs represent a significant attempt to integrate education with work. Students typically divide their time between classroom and work place, alternating school terms or dividing days. Sometimes the work is designed to complement their learning experiences. School and employers collaborate in selecting and evaluating students and in blending program content. In practice, the relationship between schooling and work varies enormously. Typically learning is entirely on the job at the work site, in clerical jobs.

The most common attraction of such programs for participating employers is that they provide a source of future staff. A majority of firms believe that at least one-third of the participants will join the firm. The advantages of evaluating staff in a work situation are considered particularly important, although sometimes line managers do not understand this value. The flexibility of these students has been noted, as has the advantage of achieving subsidization when that is available. One estimate placed the numbers in this program at 200,000 for fiscal 1979, about four times the number enrolled in OJT for the same period. These programs are a tribute to the initiative of local school systems and the receptivity of American business.

One constraint is the investment that is necessary to make the program effective, rather than just the performance of routine work. They may also involve considerable staff time in planning. Despite the advantages of these programs, many employers do not know about them and others are not in areas where programs have been established. Under the Vocational Education Act of 1963, funds are available for program development, to reimburse employers for added OJT, and as payment and compensation to student workers. The large number of participating establishments, over 60 percent, indicates that a major expansion into new companies is not likely. Nor do those currently involved foresee a major expansion of existing programs.

Short of some outside intervention or new initiative, cooperative education will undoubtedly remain about the same size for the immediate future. But it demonstrates that under the proper circumstances large numbers of businesses are willing to assume a role in training the young.

The efforts currently underway by business to accept a greater role in the training of the young are important because they demonstrate that such a role is not incompatible with the effective operation of a business. In fact, they are an integral part of a larger effort that most large American companies make to provide training and development support. A recent survey indicated that 75 percent of all companies with over 500 employees provided some in-house courses for employees, 89 percent had tuition aid or refund programs, and 74 percent authorized some of their employees to take outside courses. The median employee expenditure was $16, with 6 percent of the companies spending over $100 per employee. Training for new workers was estimated to account for 10 percent of budgeted training expenditures, while one in ten firms reported expenditures of 50 percent or more to train new workers.

But it is also true that expenditures are modest and that companies are hesitant to engage in training unless it provides a demonstrable return. As we examine federal efforts to implement OJT programs, it will be wise to keep in mind the role assigned to such programs within private firms.

Despite untold efforts and large sums of money, attempts to develop a successful system of OJT for school leavers have not reached fruition. The commitment of the designers of the Manpower Development and Training Act (MDTA) and the Comprehensive Employment and Training Act (CETA) has not yet been realized. In large part the history of American manpower policy since the 1960s can be characterized as a vain attempt to establish OJT programs that would work. The nagging possibility remains that the approach is wrong, perhaps doomed to failure. Later we will describe the highly successful German and Japanese programs of OJT. But first it will be useful to understand the difficulties of establishing OJT American style.

MDTA STARTS IT

As described above, the Manpower Development and Training Act (MDTA) from its inception had a dual focus, supporting both institutional training programs and on-the-job training carried out by local employers.[3] Despite the preference of Labor Department officials as well as congressional sponsors for OJT, initially most of the training was institutionally based classroom instruction. The expectations of Congress that one-third of all training slots would be OJT placements were not met during the first year of operation, when only 6 percent of the slots resulted in OJT placements. This percentage rose to 12 percent in 1964 and 19 percent in 1965. It became clear that promoting OJT was considerably more difficult than had been anticipated.

A major attempt to promote OJT resulted from a joint Department of Labor–Department of Health, Education, and Welfare–Office of Economic Opportunity team, which visited 30 cities in 1966. Using Jobs Now, a highly successful Chicago based OJT program, as a model, they developed the Concentrated Employment Program (CEP), which established comprehensive service centers in poverty areas. These centers performed outreach and intake, work orientation, referral to job training, and job placement. They were viewed as an important link between MDTA and local employers who would be willing to sponsor OJT programs.

The efforts to spur private sector OJT reached to the White House as well. President Lyndon Johnson, using the persuasive power of his office, met with business leaders and urged them to redouble their efforts to create OJT programs. The result was the creation of the National Alliance for Business (NAB), which provided a national office and began working to encourage national corporations to develop OJT programs. While this program did result in the involvement of a number of large companies, the results never reached the initial expectations. The NAB remains in existence and continues to serve as a central clearinghouse and facilitator for business involvement in CETA.

By the end of 1966, OJT placements rose to almost 30 percent of the total MDTA training slots, and the outlook appeared bright. An optimistic target of 50 percent was set for the next year. However, while OJT was increasingly attractive to the Department of Labor, tightening labor markets made employers less willing to create new training slots. Another factor undermining the OJT effort was the decision to target two-thirds of all CETA slots to the disadvantaged. This shift to the disadvantaged may well have triggered the demise of OJT. It should be pointed out that the gains that had been made in developing OJT slots for the most part did not involve the disadvantaged. After 1966, the percentage of OJT slots no longer increased as in the past.

OJT UNDER CETA

Again with the enactment of the Comprehensive Employment and Training Act in 1973, ambitious plans were made to develop private sector OJT placements. Whether or not these plans could have been successful, the legislation also contained a recognition in Title VI that a program of public sector jobs was needed also. In the face of depressed economic conditions, which made it difficult to locate OJT placements, the number of public sector jobs continued to rise, while the number of OJT placements decreased.

In a review of private sector involvement under CETA in 1978, Leonard Lecht noted the relatively small amount of money going to OJT programs.[4] He notes the drop off in funding from 1975 to 1978, as public sector jobs were increasing. In fact, Lecht attributes the fall-off in OJT funding to the increased funding of public sector jobs. Doubtless an interplay between the difficulty of finding OJT placements in a period of decreased economic activity and the ease of creating temporary public sector placements is responsible.

In 1977, with the enactment of the Youth Employment Demonstration Projects Act (YEDPA), a new effort to encourage employers to hire youth was undertaken.[5] One particular experiment within the Youth Incentive Entitlement Pilot Projects (YIEPP) program deserves particular attention[6] The authorizing legislation permitted prime sponsors to provide a subsidy of up to 100 percent of the youth's private sector wages. All but one prime sponsor chose to subsidize private sector jobs at 100 percent, for fear that lesser subsidies would require special rules and regulations and discourage perspective employers. Other efforts were made to eliminate the paperwork costs for a participating company. Despite the fact that over half of the work sponsors were private companies, 80 percent of the job hours were with public and nonprofit agencies, while only 20 percent were with private businesses. This resulted from the fact that the participating businesses were generally small and only accepted one or two youths at a time, while public and non-profit sponsors typically employed two to five enrollees. The youths assigned to private businesses worked most commonly as clerks, food service workers, building maintenance and repair personnel, and sales-persons.

To further test the impact of subsidies on participation by private employers, a special experiment was undertaken at two program sites. In Detroit, two groups of employers were offered subsidies of 100 percent and 75 percent, respectively. In Baltimore two groups were offered subsidies at 100 percent and 50 percent, respectively. The rate of participation corresponded to the rate of subsidy. While participation at the 100 percent subsidy level was 18 percent, participation at 75 percent was 10 percent, and at 50 percent was at 5 percent. The bulk of these placements were in small businesses, which reduced the possibility that they would lead to career positions. More often than not they reflected the desire of an individual entrepreneur to accept a "free helper" to perform sevices that might otherwise be done by himself or an hourly helper. According to William Grinker, the former head of the Manpower Demonstration Research Corporation, these results point to a relatively modest employer demand for poor, primarily minority 16–19 year olds, even at very high levels of subsidy and low employer costs.[7]

YEDPA programs suffered the same difficulties in placing their participants as the CETA programs that had preceded them. Except for its expansion of the Job Corps, which had already proven its ability to place youth successfully, its components had poor placement records. The demonstration projects, with their emphasis on keeping youth in school, hearkened back to the in-school approach of vocational education. They promoted credentialing for youth who had already rejected such efforts. YEDPA, then, while it focused attention on youth as a target for concern, was driven to in-school classes and credentialing rather than the more difficult and frustrating task of achieving placements for students in jobs with a future. As Robert Taggart, former head of the Youth Office, has noted, there is a strong reluctance on the part of the private sector to become involved with young people.[8] As Table 4.1 indicates, the proportion of youth in OJT programs has been low.

Table 4.1
Percentage of Youth in OJT, 1978

Age	YETP	Title II-B (Formerly, Title I)
Under 16	2	0
16–19	3	11
20–21	10	22
22–24	—	21

Source: Robert Taggart, "Lessons for Program Experience," in U.S. Vice President's Task Force on Youth Employment, *A Review of Youth Employment Problems, Programs and Policies,* Vol. 3 (Washington, D.C.: Government Printing Office, 1980).

In response to the growing awareness that the private sector was disappearing from CETA, a new title was added to the reauthorization of CETA that took place in 1978. The National Alliance for Business was active in working for and helping to implement Title VII, which was entitled, "Private Sector Opportunities for the Economically Disadvantaged." It established demonstration projects to test a variety of approaches to increase the involvement of the private sector in employment and training activities, with particular emphasis on increasing the employment opportunities for the economically disadvantaged. An important innovation was the provision of funds to enable the prime sponsors to establish private industry councils (PICs) to assist in the development of private sector opportunities.

The private industry councils (PICs) became the centerpiece of Title VII, which came to be referred to as the Private Sector Initiative Program (PSIP). PICs were given authority to plan and oversee expenditure of Title VII funds. They have developed in a variety of ways. An evaluation of 16 PICs found that they fit into three distinctive categories: (1) change agents that focused on effecting systemic changes in employment and training activities; (2) program operators that followed the previous CETA experience in establishing training programs, usually with a strong classroom component; and (3) single-purpose units that concentrated on some particular operation like an employment transition center for vocational exploration.[9]

These programs were small when compared to the comprehensive training programs funded by Titles II-B and C. Even by 1981, when CETA had been reduced, PSIP represented only about an eighth of the resources in Titles II-B and C. For the most part the PICs carried out programs of classroom training and OJT similar to those already developed under CETA. The key difference in PIC programming was in the management of programs with a clear thrust toward better needs assessment and careful design and management of the programs. This resulted in part from the predominance of business leaders on the PICs, who tended to make them operate like boards of directors of a corporation.

The evaluation of the PICs conclude that, while they perform a valuable role, it would be unwise to force them into a uniform mold throughout the country. They also recommend maintaining primary responsibility in the government entity, the prime sponsors.

Among the programmatic innovations attributed to the PICs are performance-based contracting, simplified contracting, customized training programs, employer consortia, and guaranteed placement. Performance-based training typically allowed for a partial payment of a contract's full cost with the balance paid when contractor met specified placement goals. Simplified contracting, allowing for the reduction in paperwork and documentation, was not widespread. In approximately half of the training sites, customized training was emphasized, although it was often difficult to implement. This involved the development of a training program to meet a specific need of an employer. For example, in one PIC a firm worked with the PIC to develop a training program for training individuals as photocopy repair people. In five of the sites consortia arrangements were developed among employers in similar firms who had common training needs. In Los Angeles, for example, several trade associations in the electronics area have worked to develop joint programs. In three sites, employers made commitments to hire successful graduates, although in most sites PICs shied away from such an approach.

The PICs represent, then, a recognition of the importance of involving the private sector in training and employment, but they are plagued by the ambiguities and legacies of CETA. Like the earlier effort to reorganize by moving from MDTA to CETA, the basic program orientation defines the bounds of program success. The structure of the program emphasizes classroom training for the most disadvantaged at considerable expense without creating a viable mechanism for moving them into the job market. Private sector involvement has still not focused on the reorientation of the training function within business to place a new emphasis on skill training for young workers and in the firm.

PROBLEMS WITH OJT AMERICAN STYLE

American attempts to legislate OJT have not been encouraging. In Lecht's in-depth study of nine prime sponsors to determine what factors led to greater private sector involvement, three of the four factors related to the inadequacy of the relationship between the prime sponsors and the employers.[10] The atmosphere of suspicion between business and government within the United States is a basic given. It means that any involvement with government is looked upon with trepidation and foreboding. This generalized feeling is even stronger when focused on CETA. Many parts of the business community perceived CETA as an inefficient, make-work approach to job training over which they have no control and little effect. Among the factors cited as encouraging private sector involvement are: sensitivity to employers' needs by effective outreach and cutting through bureaucratic red tape; innovative use of trade associations, private firms, and unions in the placement process; and active links with employers through such means as chambers of commerce. It is clear that the relationship between government and the private sector has needed bolstering.

Another factor cited by Lecht and in fact noted throughout the descriptions of MDTA and CETA is the general economic climate and the overall labor market. Youth employment only appears as a problem when overall demand for labor is not high. In a thriving economy, youth, who tend to be at the lower end of the job queue, find it less difficult to obtain entry into the labor market. Conversely, it is hardest to establish new programs and involve employers in new approaches when the economy is poor and the supply of labor is abundant. Efforts to establish OJT American style have been plagued by the fact that they have attempted to respond to the greatest needs of youth when employers have the least need for workers.

A third factor in the difficulty of involving business in OJT programs has been their focus on aiding the disadvantaged. The greatest success of OJT, in fact, the only time that OJT accounted for a growing number of placements was before the emphasis on aid to the disadvantaged. MDTA began as a program to aid workers displaced by automation and only later developed its emphasis on the disadvantaged. Appeals to business to perform a social duty to hire the disadvantaged constantly run up against the basic profit-making instinct of business, which favors recruitment of the ablest workers. By focusing on disadvantage as the central condition of qualification, CETA ensures that it will not be generally successful in obtaining private sector placements. Social conscience does not serve as a major motivating force in day-to-day business decisions. A survey by the U.S. Chamber of Commerce indicates that only 13 percent of business firms have used CETA, and these do not regard it as a quality source.[11] A rare corporate statement in support of CETA was made by Andrew Pelletier, chairman and president of Mack Trucks, who testified before Congress that CETA can be made more effective by links to the private sector and that a college education is not a prerequisite to corporate success.[12]

The fourth factor is the emergence of a youth labor market in which employers are hesitant to hire individuals below their mid-twenties into career positions. In one survey conducted as early as 1970, 80–90 percent of the employers preferred workers over 22 to those under 22 even for low-level jobs.[13] This is particularly true of the large firms but seems to have affected middle-sized and small firms as well. This phenomenon is discussed in some depth in Chapter 1, but particular attention is given here to two related factors: the negative attitude toward youth, expressed by businessmen; and their unwillingness, when they hire youth, to invest in training them.

Paul Barton has suggested that the growing proportion of corporate decision makers whose sons and daughters get college degrees has influenced the social minimum age for entering adult employment.[14] What's good enough for the sons and daughters of corporate decision makers is good enough for American youth. Whether that is the actual basis for the attitudes of corporate decision makers is secondary to the recognition that, indeed, corporate managers do not view youth as potential career employees.

Former Vice President Mondale's Task Force on Youth Employment coordinated a series of roundtables to determine private sector perspectives on youth employment problems and programs.[15] Over 130 private businesses were represented, including 77 of the largest American corporations. Separate meetings were also held with 60 major national corporations and Washington-based business associations. Six White House briefings were held for a total of 56 local business persons. The major findings of these meetings were:

1. Business is distressed by the quality of individuals in the youth market, particularly by their inability to read and write.
2. A widening gap is perceived between the complexity of skills needed in entry-level jobs and the skills of youth.
3. The schools are still viewed as the primary channel for bringing youth into the world of business.
4. Business prefers to do its own skills training but is willing to work with schools and community organizations in this area.

These findings are buttressed by other studies and were anticipated in a study conducted in the early 1970s. The Office of Policy Research and Evaluation of the Department of Labor commissioned a study to find out "the bases of employer reluctance to hire people under 21 for career entry work."[16] That study of 42 large industrial corporations, involving personal interviews with corporate executives, verified these attitudes. They could, however, detect no empirical evidence to support these attitudes, nor did they detect any willingness on the part of corporate executives to study the relative performance of those under

21 as compared to those over 21. Moreover, they all assigned a low priority to youth employment as a social concern. Personnel directors were often involved in improving hiring of minorities and women but found no basis for providing a similar focus for youth.

Their perceptions of youth included beliefs that youth had highly inaccurate ideas about the world of work; that youth are less well trained and less experienced in basic work etiquette than adults; that youth are less stable, more erratic, and more mobile; that those coming from the public schools do not possess basic literacy, communication, and mathematics skills; and that youth are more militant, undisciplined, and likely to advocate and accept representation by unions.

Given these beliefs, it is no wonder that they are not eager to hire youth. They are not overly concerned about youth unemployment and in fact tend to question the accuracy and interpretation of youth employment statistics. They resist the idea of corporations making special efforts to hire youth, lest they impair their own earnings and profitability. The study found that "corporations generally have not developed specific youth employment policies" because they "have not identified youth hiring, or the lack of it, as a substantial problem on the basis of either internal needs or external social persuasion."[17]

HOPEFUL SIGNS

Some hopeful signs in the last few years have indicated that the private sector is becoming more conscious of the need to address the problem of youth employment directly. The Committee for Economic Development, a group composed largely of presidents and board chairmen of corporations and presidents of universities adopted a statement in January 1978 on "Jobs for the Hard-to-Employ, New Directions for a Public-Private Partnership."[18] That statement favored a strong national commitment to high employment, matching the number of people seeking jobs and providing adequate opportunities for training. It sought to expand existing private sector programs, strengthen organization mechanisms for mobilizing private sector involvement, increase incentives to private employers to hire the hard-to-employ, and improve approaches to the problems of particular groups. That statement acknowledged the fact that youth (16–24) account for nearly half of the total unemployment.

Local groups of business leaders have also made some efforts in this new direction. Capitalizing on the effective work of some local groups, the CETA legislation was amended in 1978 to include a provision to develop private industry councils at the local level. A few, like the one in New York City, have been quite successful in locating jobs and developing training programs.

Another group that deserves particular mention for its efforts in the area of youth employment is the New York City Partnership. Since its founding in 1979, it has focused on youth employment and, in the wake of cutbacks in government-funded job programs during the summer of 1981, launched a major campaign to identify summer jobs for New York City youth. It is now expanding its interest to longer-term projects.

Individual corporations and industrywide groups have also undertaken some especially successful efforts. The Security Pacific Bank in Los Angeles has developed the Skills Training Educational Program (STEP). STEP is a community service project, training high school students and some adults for entry-level jobs in the banking industry. Participating educational institutions hope to provide students with an opportunity to learn practical jobs skills in a business environment, where they are taught by "banker/teachers" who have access to the latest banking business practices.

STEP offers some 100 classes taught at 30 bank branches and offices throughout the state. After regular banking hours, bank offices are transformed into learning laboratories, and bank employees become teachers with the full support and approval of their employer. They conduct courses on their own time and are paid at teaching wages by the local school districts. To qualify they must have five years of bank experience or three years of experience with a related college degree and take a 60-hour teacher training course.

While about half of the classes concentrate on basic teller instruction, the remaining classes offer a wide variety of practical skills such as bank reconciling, data entry and word processing. Approximately 25 percent of the program's graduates are hired by the bank, with additional hundreds hired by other banks. In addition to providing a steady flow of new employees, it has proven a powerful public relations tool.

Two conclusions are possible from the dismal record of involving the private sector in the United States in expanding OJT efforts. One is that progress in this direction is impossible; the other is that the emphasis has been wrong. While many specialists adhere to the former view, evidence pointing to the more hopeful alternative has been cited.

The successes that have been achieved in developing private sector training placements in the United States and abroad suggest that options are open to governments that want to contribute to the employment of youth. The process of involving private businesses in manpower strategies has been hopelessly simplified. Businesses are asked to bring new individuals into their work place, create jobs for them, and consider hiring them permanently without any long-range commitment from the government that the plan will continue and that the investment of company resources will lead to a productive relationship.

The disruption to organizations, particularly the larger ones, of hiring trainees, is formidable. Yet the large organizations are the ones whose resources justify the establishment of a formal training program. They must be convinced that the investment in such a program will bring a suitable return. It most certainly will not unless a long-range program is developed to integrate the trainees into the company effectively.

Although government policy has had a superficial appeal and appearance as if it were opening its doors to private involvement in job programs, in fact it has been both naive and half-hearted. Nor has it made extraordinary efforts to involve business in planning for policy implementation at the local level. Even the private industry councils, perhaps the largest step in this direction, have left much to be desired.

The overriding fact of private sector involvement in the United States is that it occurred in spite of CETA. The utter failure of CETA to gain the confidence of the private sector led in large part to the substitution of the Jobs Training Partnership Act of 1982. Despite the increased influence of PICs in the new legislation, it does not propose a programmatic solution. All evidence suggests that no major breakthroughs in involving the private sector in training programs are imminent.

NOTES

1. The material in the next several pages is based in large part on two studies conducted by Seymour Lusterman and Harriet Gorlin for the Conference Board: Seymour Lusterman, *Education in Industry* (New York: Conference Board, 1977); and Seymour Lusterman and Harriet Gorlin, *Educating Students for Work: Some Business Roles* (New York: The Conference Board, 1980).

2. For discussion of apprenticeship programs on an international basis, *see* Beatrice Reubens, *Policies for Apprenticeship* (Paris: OECD, 1979).

3. For a description of the legislative history and surrounding developments, *see* Joseph Ball, "The Implementation of Federal Manpower Policy, 1961–1971" (Ph.D. diss., Columbia University, 1972).

4. Leonard Lecht, *Involving Private Employers in Local CETA Programs* (New York: Conference Board, 1979).

5. Andrew Hahn, "Taking Stock of YEDPA: The Federal Youth Employment Initiatives," *Youth and Society* 2, no. 2 (1979): 237–261.

6. These efforts are described in Joseph Ball et al., *The Quality of Work in the Youth Entitlement Demonstration* (New York: Manpower Demonstration Research Corporation, 1980); and William Diaz et al., *The Youth Entitlement Demonstration* (New York: Manpower Demonstration Research Corporation, 1980).

7. William Grinker, Executive Director, Manpower Demonstration Research Corporation, Testimony before the Labor Subcommittee of the Senate Labor and Human Resources Committee, March 24, 1981.

8. Robert Taggart, "Lessons from Program Experience," in U.S. Vice President's Task Force on Youth Employment, *A Review of Youth Employment Problems, Programs and Policies*, vol. 3 (Washington, D.C.: Government Printing Office, 1980).

9. Public/Private Ventures, *Private Sector Initiatives Program: Documentation and Assessment of CETA Title VII Implementation* (Philadelphia: Public/Private Ventures, 1982).

10. Lecht, *Involving Private Employers*.

11. U.S. Chamber of Commerce, *A Survey of Federal Employment and Training Programs* (Washington, D.C.: National Chamber Forecast and Survey Center, September 1978).

12. Andrew Pelletier, Statement before the Subcommittee on Elementary, Secondary and Vocational Education of the House Committee on Education and Labor, January 1980.

13. Richard B. Freeman, *Why Is There a Youth Labor Market Problem?* (Cambridge, Mass.: National Bureau of Economic Research, 1979. Prentice-Hall, 1980).

14. Paul Barton, "Youth Transition to Work: The Problem and Federal Policy," in Anderson and Sawhill, *Youth Employment*.

15. Summary of Mondale task force interview with employers (Washington, D.C.: Vice President Mondale's Task Force, 1980).

16. Manpower Institute, *Study of Corporate Youth Employment Policies and Practices* (Washington, D.C.: Manpower Institute, 1973).

17. Ibid.

18. Committee for Economic Development, *Jobs for the Hard-to-Employ: New Directions for a Public-Private Partnership* (New York: Committee for Economic Development, 1978).

CHAPTER 5

OJT Foreign Style

DYNAMIT NOBEL

Dynamit Nobel is a multinational corporation with German origins.[1] It has plants in many countries and major locations in Germany and like other German companies has maintained a continuing commitment to apprenticeship training since the middle of the last century. One of its plants is located in the industrial city of Cologne. The plant facilities are like those of any large progressive industrial corporation, replete with staff cafeteria serving high-quality meals. This location is special because it is the site of the major center for training apprentices for Dynamit Nobel.

The training center is not plush, but is clean and ample in size. It is a cross between a factory and an office building. In one corner of the entranceway is a scale model of a chemical plant which is used in instruction but the model would probably be too expensive for an American vocational school. Inside there are students and instructors just like there would be in a vocational high school back in the states, but the differences are striking.

The premises consist of a series of chemical, electrical, and mechanical workshops. The look is more of a factory than a school. The students are hard at work doing practical things: fashioning their projects in the machine shops, undertaking experiments in chemistry, and completing their electrical wiring projects. The instructors, while selected for their inclination and ability as teachers, were themselves workers in the factories. They know what they are teaching from practical experience and from continuing contact with what is happening in the plants.

During 1981, 192 apprentices began their studies at the center in Cologne, representing 24 different specializations. Some typical titles are sheet metal worker, lathe operator, figure locksmith, technical drafts-man, pipe installer, and steel molder. Sometimes closely related disci-plines receive instruction together. But the instruction is focused on workshops and producing products, rather than abstractions. One day a week students attend a vocational high school, where together with others from local apprenticeship programs they receive more formal in-struction. The *Duales System* requires them to attend such a school for three years, through the age of 18.

The 24 defined categories of study at Dynamit Nobel are a few of the over 400 defined categories within the German apprenticeship pro-gram. Each of these categories has a curriculum that has been agreed to by a study group convened by the Federal Vocational Training Insti-tute and comprising representation from the employers associations, the trade unions, and the *Lander* (the equivalent of our state governments, which are responsible for education). But it is up to each company run-ning an apprenticeship program to implement that curriculum. Repre-sentatives from the local chambers of commerce and industry will test the apprentices. They also have the obligation to oversee the programs and investigate any complaints about the programs. The trade unions also will make sure that the apprentices are treated well, since they are covered by the collective bargaining agreements.

While apprentices come within the collective bargaining agreement, they are not considered workers. The companies do not pay social se-curity taxes for them, and the apprentices have no right to retention after completing the apprenticeship. They do receive a stipend, which typically starts at 25 percent of a beginning worker's salary.

I asked Mr. Friedberg, the director of the training center, why Dy-namit Nobel runs such a program. Mr. Friedberg is himself an engi-neer, although he enjoys teaching courses in the center. He explained that some calculations had been made, and the costs of the apprentice-ship are estimated at DM 18,000 per year per apprentice. The figure includes all training costs and stipends and deducts from these the value of productive labor. That means if 200 apprentices are begun each year and they last approximately three years, the costs per year would be DM 10.8 million. Why does Dynamit Nobel make such an expenditure? The answer is simple: this is the way new skilled workers are recruited. German companies accept the costs and responsibility of training their workers. This way they are sure that the workers know how to do it their way, on the most modern equipment. If they were sent to voca-tional school, they'd have to be trained at the company anyway. Be-sides, it's part of the accepted corporate social obligation to participate in the training of the young. The programs are well known and attract a high caliber of student. Companies are investing in their own fu-tures.

Most large German companies have training centers similar to the one at Dynamit Nobel, which supplement the training that occurs on the floor of the factory. Smaller companies often cooperate to establish common facilities.

THE GERMAN APPRENTICESHIP SYSTEM

The historical accident that preserved the German apprenticeship system while those of most other industrialized countries were falling into disuse, has already been alluded to. The *Duales System*, established in 1897 and emphasizing both practical training on site and theoretical training in school, has survived and prospered.[2] In 1971, 68 percent of all working people born in 1918 or later had completed an apprenticeship. From among those who had completed specialized training or higher education, 50 percent had completed apprenticeships. Today it is the apprenticeship system that places secondary school leavers, typically at age 15, upon graduation from the lower secondary school. It is accepted as an integral part of German preparatory life, without the stigma attached to apprenticeships in the United Kingdom and France.

Perhaps the most striking aspect of the *Duales System* is its acceptance as a legitimate path for young people to follow. Companies, too, view the apprenticeship system as costly but worthwhile for recruiting individuals into the ranks of skilled labor and beyond. Individuals who complete apprenticeships may continue on in school for technical degrees or go back into a university track. In fact, in times of strong demand for labor, companies have objected to the frequency with which their well-trained skilled workers choose to pursue educational options, rather than continuing on directly with the company. Given the substantial investment that top companies make in these positions, an estimated DM 50,000 over the three-year life of the apprenticeship, this is understandable.

The German apprenticeship system, along with similar systems in Austria and Switzerland, is a system of on-the-job training for school leavers that developed from the medieval apprenticeship system but has achieved a distinctive character. While its form is similar to apprenticeship systems in the United States and France, its comprehensiveness makes it distinctive. The United Kingdom has attempted to emulate the system, but it has not achieved the breadth of the German system.

Its key is a universal approach, which more or less guarantees to all school leavers from the *hauptschule*, with a general certificate, a placement in on-the-job training, which is based upon a formal apprenticeship contract between the individual and the employer. Once an individual decides to enter a particular field, a vocational counselor functioning under the Bundesanstalt fur Arbeit (Federal Employment

Institute) recommends actual placements in companies or schools. While the program is aimed at those graduating with a general certificate, school leavers not attaining this qualification may find an apprenticeship, as may students with higher qualifications. The total number of apprenticeships is quite large, for example, during 1979 there were 1,644,600 apprentices, representing 39.8 percent of the population between the ages of 15 and 19. The new training contracts entered that year covered 62.3 percent of the population between 15 and 16.

For 1979 the placements made through the apprenticeship system were distributed as follows: industry and commerce, 45.5 percent; crafts, 41.1 percent; agriculture, 2.8 percent; public service, 3.3 percent; free professions, domestic science, maritime shipping, 7.3 percent. The 25 occupations with the greatest number of apprentices in order of their importance are motor vehicle mechanic, salesman, hairdresser, industrial clerk, electrical fitter, office clerk, clerk in wholesale and foreign trade, machine fitter, saleswoman in foodstuffs, salesman in retail trades, bank clerk, joiner, painter and varnisher, bricklayer, doctor's receptionist, gas and water fitter, baker, dentist's receptionist, butcher, toolmaker, fitter, plant fitter, cook, farm worker, specialized assistant in tax consultancy and auditing. This list indicates the breadth of the placements. Some of the apprenticeships, particularly those in large industrial and commercial enterprises, involve specially developed training courses at company schools, while others rely upon direct supervision on the job. Companies with limited resources are encouraged to work together to sponsor common training facilities where necessary and appropriate.

Sometimes the quality of placements is criticized. Some commentators have noted that when the number of training places increased in the late 1970s so did the proportions of those in the trades of hairdresser and baker. These apprenticeships are viewed as cheap labor because of the high apprenticeship productivity and low training investment. It is pointed out that many small tradesmen retain more apprentices than they could possible hire. While this criticism is certainly justified, it must also be pointed out that in a period in which the need for training places increased, the small shops performed a valuable function by providing places for young persons who otherwise would have been without them. And many of those completing such apprenticeships found work in other fields in part because of their training experience.

The wide range of apprenticeships presents a difficult problem of quality control. The Bundesinstitut fur Berufsbildung (Federal Vocational Training Institute), which is responsible for developing curricula for all categories of apprenticeship, has attempted to upgrade the content in recent years and to ensure that the content contains sufficient general and theoretical material. Since 1969, most curricula have been reviewed by tripartite committees convened by the Federal Vocational Training Institute and including representatives of the employers, the trade unions and the *Lander*. The effectiveness of the Federal Vocational Training Institute in developing curricula that are distributed nationally and represent compromises over diverse views is one of the outstanding strengths of the system.

In addition to the training at the employers' work sites, all *Lander* require at least one day per week of vocational training in school, and some *Lander* require two days per week. All those completing apprenticeships must be examined by the local chamber of commerce and industry, and the trade unions take an active part in quality control. Some *Lander* have recently instituted an initial year of training in a vocational school before certain apprenticeships, while certain technical skills are being taught in vocational school programs. These incursions on the *Duales System* tend to be resisted by the employers, however, who prefer to take direct responsibility for the training of apprentices. There is an increasing tendency to use training centers, such as the one described above, in conjunction with training at the work site.

The relationship of the *Duales System* to the total labor market system supervised by the Federal Vocational Training Institute and in particular the Division of Labor Market Policy became prominent in the late 1970s. Since the apprenticeship program is relied upon by the vast majority of those leaving the *hauptschule*, when general unemployment increases the demands for apprenticeship places is greater than ever. The Division of Labor Market Policy took an active role during the late 1970s in encouraging employers to increase the number of training places. The Training Places Promotion Act enacted in 1976 served as a spur, but appeals were also made directly to companies. The increase in training places helped avoid the sharply rising rates of youth unemployment that surfaced in the rest of Western Europe. By encouraging companies to increase the number of their training places, a temporary expedient was found. Of course, the problems faced by 18 year olds completing the apprenticeships and older workers remained. But the ability of the government to use the existing training system to absorb additional young people, without creating expensive new government programs, was a striking contrast to other European countries. Employers were merely asked to do more of what they had always done.

During the 1970s, as youth unemployment rose in Europe, the German, Austrian, and Swiss apprenticeship programs were often held up as models for the other European countries. Yet many Europeans, the British and French particularly, criticize the apprenticeship system for its narrow emphasis on job-specific training. Doesn't this deprive a youngster of the further education needed for long-term economic and social success? The Germans counter this criticism by emphasizing the flexibility of the system, which allows for movement from one stream to another. The phenomenon of apprentices moving into higher education is often cited, although this has been curtailed recently as the job market has become tighter.

The argument made against the German apprenticeship system doubtless has some validity. But it should be remembered that when school leavers enter the *Duales System* in Germany, a similar proportion of young people in France and the United Kingdom are entering the labor force or specialized vocational education. They too must make the kinds of decisions that new apprentices must make.

In fact, Germany is distinctive in the small percentage of students who actually enter the work force. The argument could be made that by providing a training experience the German system provides a considerably broader experience than that received by individuals who are forced to enter the work force, and even those entering vocational education systems, which in both France and the United Kingdom can be quite narrow. It might be argued further that the opportunity to receive training in the work place is a broadening aspect of the German vocational system, which other countries seek through a variety of ad hoc measures.

The *Duales System*, then, has resulted in a unique orientation emphasizing OJT for those in the 15–18-year category. Apart from those young who go on in school aiming for higher education and the small percentage who attend vocational schools, all secondary school leavers in Germany enter this OJT program. The organized comprehensive system is quite different from the informal and haphazard system in the United States and other countries used for moving secondary school leavers into the world of work. This supportive system focuses responsibility for job counseling in the public employment service and places most young people in OJT placements in firms. Approximately two-thirds of the apprenticeships are advertised, while one-third are still filled by word of mouth. The three-year apprenticeship is carefully regulated by an apprenticeship contract, which is supervised by the local chamber of commerce and industry and monitored by the trade union.

In addition, the individual must attend vocational school at least one day per week. At the end of the apprenticeship the trainee is ordinarily offered a full-time position. A large percentage of the trainees stay on, and statistics indicate that three years after completion of the apprenticeship approximately 50 percent of the apprentices are still with the firms that originally hired them. The *Duales System* represents a unique blend of government, employer, and trade union cooperation. But the central responsibility rests with the individual firm. It is a sterling example of creativity in managing the transition from school to work and providing the structured contact with the adult world that other industrialized countries seek but have such a hard time realizing.

JAPAN

If Germany has evolved a highly organized system for training young people and helping in their transition to the world of work that is centered on the individual firm, the Japanese have evolved a system that is the firm.[3] Without the existence of special categories of apprenticeship or government or association oversight, Japanese companies have come to accept the responsibility for training young people within their firms.

Japanese companies have extensive OJT programs for orienting and training young workers. These programs are part of a larger system that encourages private companies to hire workers at a young age and provides a variety of training opportunities as part of a lifetime employment system. Data in the mid–1970s indicated that the ratio of jobs to junior high school graduates was 5.9 to 1; for senior high graduates, 3.4 to 1; and slightly less for college graduates.

A key element in understanding the disposition of Japanese companies to hire young workers and invest in their training is the steeply graduated system of seniority wages. The salaries of young workers are low, since it is anticipated that they do not have great needs. As they mature, marry, and have children their salaries increase, largely on the basis of time of service. Length of service is the single greatest determinant of compensation, with differentials among education groups minimal, especially during the initial period of employment. For example, between 1965 and 1975 salaries of senior high graduates rose from 71.4 percent to 84.2 percent of those of university graduates.

The seniority wage system provides monetary incentives to hire young workers and retire older workers. And in fact companies have been more eager to retire older workers in periods of cutback than to fire new workers. Until recently a retirement age of 55 was generally observed despite the fact that life expectancy and realistic working life has lengthened since the Japanese practice was initiated at the turn of the century. Recent efforts to extend the retirement age to 60 are one indication of the difficulties encountered by older workers. While most industrialized countries have adopted measures to help younger workers, it is interesting to note that Japan has instituted measures to assist older workers. The employment system in Japan has resulted in a very high demand for young workers and a continuing competition for young workers, who are considered flexible and inexpensive.

In order to understand the basis of the Japanese system of OJT for young workers it is necessary to understand the philosophy of Japanese management as well as the historical context in which the present system has developed. During the feudal age, the apprenticeship system was in wide use, but as industry developed during the second half of the nineteenth century a different system of training developed. The Meiji government, which made great strides toward industrialization, struggled with the problem of training from its inception. When foreign experts were brought in to assist in the construction and operation of new factories, Japanese understudies were attached to them to learn their jobs. The government established model enterprises where workers could learn skills and then move into the private sector. But the great demand for skilled workers resulted in considerable mobility for trained workers.

In the face of a highly mobile force, individual enterprises developed their own strategies for the recruitment and training of workers, while the government focused its efforts on promoting institutional training of technicians, engineers, and supervisory personnel. Some of the larger firms adopted policies of recruiting inexperienced youths and providing training within their factories.

In the period between World War I and World War II, the government sought to provide institutional training for craftsmen, but was generally not successful. Schools were generally viewed as a means to higher social status and not as a path for craftsmen. As production processes were divided into simplified jobs, highly skilled workers became unnecessary and industry developed a system of internal training within the enterprises themselves. Factory workers were hired directly into production, and management assumed responsibility for skill acquisition. While the specific training provided nontransferable skills, companies accepted responsibility for indefinite employment.

During the 1930s the government sought to encourage the development of skilled manpower. In 1939, the government issued an order requiring employers to provide training for workers in a variety of skills. While large firms reorganized their training to comply, the demands of wartime production soon undermined the effective institutionalization of this training system.

In the post–World War II era, the government enacted a series of measures designed to encourage a coordinated system for training employees. The Labor Standards Law of 1947 was intended to protect young trainees from exploitation and at the same time to promote more systematic craftsmanship training. The Vocational Training Law of 1958 attempted for the first time to create a unified system of vocational training. Manufacturing industries were booming, and skilled labor was in demand. Young school leavers were especially valued, although inexperienced adults were also recruited. The new law emphasized the reorganization and expansion of the training activities of public institutions. During the 1960s, as the economic boom continued, most of the large firms arranged to recruit and train their own workers, while the public vocational training center graduates were going to smaller firms.

When the Vocational Training Law was revised in 1974 and 1978, the emphasis was on the provision of adequate OJT opportunities by employers. Initial training for new entrants to industry and upgrading training for those in employment were mostly left to industry. Public institutions were to provide retraining for the displaced. In summary, while the government through legislation and decrees has over the years encouraged industry to provide training and itself provided start-up training in its own factories, it has been content to allow private industry to develop their own training programs. Spurred by their own needs for skilled manpower during the early periods of industrialization and again in the post–World War II era, private companies have developed training programs for young entrants that emphasize OJT.

These programs have developed in a prevailing corporate system in which the larger firms are committed to investment in young workers as part of their overall strategy of human resources development. As one training manager suggested, "We are concerned with the development of people, not the cost involved." The employee is not hired for a particular job, but it is understood that the company will train him as the need arises. The system benefits both the worker, who receives the opportunities for development, and the firm, which is able to recoup its investment by retaining trained personnel.

This human resources orientation reflects the need for skilled workers and the successful development of the internal labor market as an adaptation to this situation. By supporting a system of lifetime employment with minimum labor mobility, companies minimize their losses of trained employees. Yet there are exceptions. In banking, women are usually recruited as secretaries who will leave work once they marry, while only men are considered career employees. Job mobility is becoming an increasing phenomenon. Statistics indicate that of those who obtained jobs in 1970, 20 percent quit within one year, 30 percent within the next three years, and an additional 20 percent within the next two years. In fact, the phenomenon of job hoppers or "straying sheep" has been considered a source of juvenile delinquency.

Some observers attribute this highly developed system of internal training with encouraging the high level of motivation of Japanese workers as exemplified by their low rate of absenteeism. Shimada points out that the system of training is an integral part of the Japanese employment system, which emphasizes the internal labor market. Since employers develop their own workers rather than purchasing skills in the labor market, they are used to providing a variety of training opportunities. Furthermore, Shimada argues, this system of training is carefully integrated with the structure of the organization and its system of promotion. This connection is indicated in Figure 1.

As can be seen from Figure 1, the internal training system is closely linked with other subsystems, such as ranks in jobs and statuses, work organization, allocation of work force, promotion, and wages. The system emphasizes not only skill development in a narrow sense, including both formal off-the-job and informal on-the-job training, but total and comprehensive personal development. This system of internal training thus reinforces the worker's motivation and organizational commitment, which are themselves fostered by the overall cultural milieu and the operation of enterprise unions.

The informal OJT is reinforced by the Japanese system of job rota-

Figure 1
An Organizational Model of Internal Training

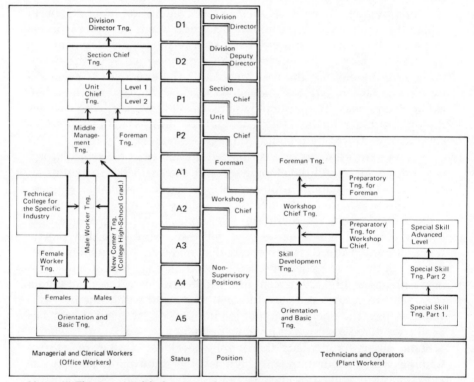

Notes: (1) This is a simplified version of an organizational chart of the system of internal training of a large firm in the steel industry.

(2) In status ranking, "D" stands for directors, "P" for principal administrators, and "A" for administrators. All usage of the words and translated expressions are the choice of the author and do not represent the official expressions of the corporation.

Source: Haruo Shimada, *The Japanese Employment System* (Tokyo: The Japan Institute of Labour, 1980), p. 19. Reprinted with permission.

tion, which results in a variety of work situations and opportunities for skill development. This system of job rotation helps reinforce the relationship of the worker to the company as opposed to a narrow commitment to a particular job or set of skills.

While the full extent of company training is difficult to summarize and it is nearly impossible to estimate the resources devoted to it, a 1974 Ministry of Labour survey devoted to on-the-job training provides an indication of the extent of company commitment to formal training programs.

Table 5.1 indicates that most large firms carry out extensive training programs in addition to informal OJT. Of those companies employing over 300 workers, more than 75 percent are providing some training programs. Over 70 percent are providing training for college students

Table 5.1
Percentage of Establishments Giving Training Programs by Size of Establishments, 1974

(in percentage)

Size of Establishment (the number of employees)	Establishments Giving Training	New Entrants to the Company				
		New School Leavers				Halfway Workers
		Semi-Total	College	High School	Middle School	
Total	41.3	64.8	70.1	66.6	54.5	26.0
1,000 and over	95.1	86.6	87.9	92.9	72.8	61.9
500 to 999	85.3	79.0	78.7	81.3	74.7	45.0
300 to 499	75.9	70.6	70.1	73.8	64.8	36.5
100 to 299	58.8	57.0	59.9	59.3	48.3	28.0
30 to 99	26.3	30.9	39.2	31.5	22.7	12.0
5 to 29	10.1	15.3	20.6	15.7	12.4	5.4

	Workers Already on the Payroll					
	Semi-Total	Production		Technical	Clerical & Sales	Managerial
		Rank & File	Foremen			
Total	22.2	20.4	29.0	24.5	10.4	21.1
1,000 and over	62.5	63.8	75.9	58.7	54.0	60.8
500 to 999	44.8	44.5	58.9	41.4	37.7	42.7
300 to 499	32.6	29.1	45.6	31.8	26.0	31.6
100 to 299	24.6	22.3	32.6	23.6	21.5	24.0
30 to 99	10.2	10.1	12.6	12.3	8.2	8.8
5 to 29	4.4	4.8	5.4	8.2	2.2	2.8

Source: Ministry of Labour, *Jigyonai Kyoikukunren Jisshi Jokyo Chosa* (Survey of Intra-Firm Vocational Training and Education), 1974. Reprinted in Haruo Shimada, *The Japanese Employment System* (Tokyo: The Japan Institute of Labour, 1980), p. 21. Reprinted with permission.

and secondary school leavers. Of course, smaller companies employing under 29 workers have much more difficulty in establishing formal training programs.

Many large Japanese companies have extensive training programs. Over 365 company-based training schools have been recognized by prefectural governments. An example, the Toden Academy of Tokyo Electric Company, was authorized in 1959. Each spring 200 junior high school graduates are taken into the three-year program, which is the equivalent of a senior high school. All the student expenses are paid, and a monthly allowance is provided. After graduation the student may enter a company-run junior college and qualify for specialized training leading to technical and managerial positions.

The elaborate training program developed by Tokyo Electric Power Company is divided into four levels: the central personnel unit; the Toden Academy; the individual departments; and individual sections. Training programs are provided by each of these levels, in addition to the comprehensive system of on-the-job training, which is fostered by the system of rotating employees among different jobs.

The personnel development department is responsible for overall planning and coordination of the company's training programs. It also has overall responsibility for supervising and controlling the training conducted in each department and section. In addition it makes arrangements for long-term training programs abroad. The Toden Academy runs university and high school divisions, which provide internal long-term training for promising individuals who will assume positions of leadership in the company. It also runs specialized technical training and managerial training programs. Departments run specialized training programs in such areas as community relations, systematization and modernization of facilities, and safe operating procedures as well as management training. They also coordinate the participation of sections in central programs and supervise sectional programs. The sections supervise OJT. They also provide group training for new employees and certain other training programs. The specific extent of training programs at these different levels is explained in Table 5.2.

While a detailed statement of the resources devoted to training is difficult to obtain, since it is considered confidential, the dedication to training and personal development is manifest. When queried about the high costs of training, the manager of training at Tokyo Electric Power Company replied that the investment in human resources, not cost, is the central issue. One wonders, however, whether the slowing of economic growth and corporate profits will not change the orientation of Japanese companies and result in a reduction in expenditures on training. In fact, despite the rhetoric of concern for personal development, without budget information it is really difficult to judge the extent of these training efforts. Such expensive programs as company high schools and universities are usually limited to a small number of individuals, and outside training is often reserved for higher-level management.

Nonetheless, the commitment to training entry-level workers is clear. The larger companies much prefer to hire individuals with broad education in prestigious schools and universities and then provide specific skills training. In fact, this commitment to internal training has undermined much of the support for vocational education within the Japanese educational system. The better students prefer to compete for the limited openings in prestigious institutions, and the companies seem to reciprocate by employing them.

Since 95 percent of all junior high school graduates go on to senior high school, Japanese companies no longer send talent scouts to rural areas in quest of "golden eggs," the junior high school graduates who would be brought directly into the company. But their youth orientation has remained. They prefer to hire younger workers, who are considered more flexible and inexpensive. This attitude is in stark contrast to that of American companies, which are increasingly inclined to hire workers who are in their middle twenties and considered more settled and mature. This attitude, of course, reflects the larger economic system and labor market. It also means that the period of instability that characterizes American youth during their late teens and early twenties is replaced by a period of general stability and training within the company. The result is the effective utilization of young workers and the establishment of both ties to the company and the social system for those school leavers not attending university.

LESSONS FROM ABROAD

In trying to analyze the success of the *Duales System* in Germany and the internal training system in Japan, the willingness of companies to become actively involved in recruiting and training youth is the single most impressive feature. While individual companies in the United Kingdom, France, the United States, and Scandinavia have highly successful training programs for secondary school graduates, the breadth and scope of the German and Japanese systems are distinctive. Two factors play critical roles: historical circumstance; and the structure of incentives to the company.

In both Germany and Japan corporate responsibility for the development of human resources has evolved over a relatively long period of time. The German adherence to the apprenticeship system is based upon a medieval system that was strengthened and changed throughout the nineteenth and twentieth centuries. The Japanese system of internal training developed at the turn of the century in response to the

TABLE 5.2
Organizational Objectives, Tokyo Electric Power Company

Name / Function	Employees Group	New Employees	Employees with Less Than Three Years Experience	Experienced Employees	Junior Management	Senior Management
Objectives		Orientation and fundamental training	Training and review of fundamental operating procedure / Improvement of customer relations		Improvement of managerial and technical skills and leadership abilities	
Personnel Development Department	Planning; Control and supervision; Accreditation; Foreign trainee program		Long-term training abroad (foreign graduate schools, or at power companies abroad); Domestic long-term training; Accreditation			
Toden Academy	University Division			The "Honka" (university core) and the "Senka" (specialized training core)		
	Technical Training Center			Electric generation-transformation, electricity transmission, thermal power, systems management, electricity distribution, technology and construction		
	High School Department		Power Electronics Course; University and technical school graduates training; English language training and correspondence course training assistance	Control Electrical School; Thermal power simulator; Systems Engineering Course; Computer training		Senior management training
	Training Department	Group training and orientation			Management training	
Individual Departments	Planning; Supervision; Cooperation and aid	Group training (Electricity distribution and transmission)	Training to establish fundamental operating procedures and knowledge	Specialist's skills; Community relations; Systematization and modernization of facilities; Safe operating procedures	Management training	Senior management training
Individual Sections	Planning the training for the section; Supervision of on-the-job training; Training of new employees	Group training of university, technical high school, and high school graduates; Training on fundamental business practice	Training to familiarize employees with fundamental procedures of each section; Safety drills; Computer training	Training of those preparing to retire; Training to upgrade technical knowledge; Training to assist in improvement and modernization of plant and facilities	Management training	Senior management training
			Aid to those engaging in independent study on their own time			

74

The names of the departments or sections which conduct training or personnel development programs are listed below, together with the functions they fulfill and their objectives. Also see the accompanying chart.

Personnel Development Department

— Overall planning and coordination of the Company's personnel development program.

— Planning and establishing a fundamental policy for the various training programs conducted at Tokyo Electric Power Company.

— Supervising and controlling the training conducted in each department and section.

— Training accreditation.

— Making arrangements for and assigning and dispatching Company employees to long-term training programs, and making arrangements for special trainees from abroad.

Toden Academy

University Division

— A "Honka" (university core division) and a "Senka" (specialized training core division), both directed toward training people to be able to assume positions of importance and responsibility within the Company.

Technical Training Center

— Training directed toward improvement of the trainee's technical knowledge and managerial capabilities.

High School Department

— Training directed toward enabling people to assume active roles in the Company and to possess the recognition of the importance of their roles and of the public nature and important societal function of the public utility company.

Training Department

— Training designed to improve operating procedures and to upgrade managers' skills.

Departmental Training

— Drawing up plans for and setting the direction of training for the entire department.

— Supervising and leading the training for each section.

— Aiding and cooperating with the training programs of Toden Academy and each section.

Section Training

— Planning and implementation of training for the section.

-- Supervising and leading on-the-job training for service personnel.

Source: "A Policy for Human Resource Development," The Tokyo Electric Power Company, Inc., pp. 2–3.

need for specialized training created by the new industrialization. Both of these systems were strengthened in the period between the wars.

Then, the end of World War II presented both countries with critical shortages of trained personnel, which required a systematic and effective means for training new skilled workers. The apprenticeship system in Germany and the internal training system in Japan became the means for developing skilled personnel in a period of labor shortage. This link between corporate need for skilled personnel and labor market shortages is particularly relevant in analyzing the failures of other industrialized countries to develop OJT programs for youth. Invariably these efforts have been mounted in times of labor abundance, when the problem of youth employment has become a politically explosive issue. During such times little incentive exists for a company to engage in human resource development. The company is more interested in measures to reduce existing personnel, and what needs exist can be met in the labor market. Since these government efforts to encourage corporate investment in human resources development occur at the worst possible time from the corporate point of view, even large subsidies do not make these programs attractive.

The second critical element in the German and Japanese systems is the monetary incentive to hire the young. In both systems young workers receive only a portion of the wages of regular workers. In Germany this results from the official designation of an apprentice as a trainee and in Japan from the seniority wage system. Especially in Germany, the high costs of training apprentices in the larger companies is a substantial burden and without the youth differential might well be considered too costly.

While the trade unions in the United States and the United Kingdom have fought such a wage differential, the unions in both Germany and Japan accept this difference, although at times controversy has developed. Recently this issue of compensation for young workers has been raised in both Sweden and the United Kingdom, where employers and unions have cooperated in establishing new programs of OJT. In December 1981, the Swedish Employers' Confederation (SAF) and the major union groups reached agreement on a program to provide jobs for 16 and 17 year olds with a stipend of 85 Swedish kroner a day, with the government reimbursing the companies at 75 Swedish kroner a day. In addition the employer paid social security and other charges.

In April 1982, the *Youth Task Group Report*, with the support of the Confederation of British Industries and the Trades Union Congress, the local educational authorities, and the Manpower Services Commission, proposed a program of full-year traineeships building upon the program of Work Experiences on Employers Premises for 16 and 17 year olds. A compromise was reached to continue stipends at the levels of the previous year with a slight upgrading, while also increasing the quality of the training. The government provides grants to companies to cover the stipends, plus additional monies to subsidize the training efforts.

While the historical basis of the German and Japanese systems and the incentive structure for hiring the young are critical, a third element of the German and Japanese system stands out. Both of these systems recruit young workers into companies in the regular course of events. The companies in a very direct sense compete with the educational systems for human resources. In fact, certainly in the Japanese case the dramatic rise in schooling has contributed to the continuing scarcity of young labor.

In contrast, the attempts of the United Kingdom, the United States, France, and Sweden to develop private sector programs have almost invariably centered on helping the disadvantaged, the school dropout, or the unemployed. Companies are asked in the name of social conscience to help with the placement of a group of individuals already labeled as failures by the educational system. Is it any wonder that companies in these countries resist involvement in programs that ask them to accept social responsibility for the least desirable workers? Surely the structure of private enterprise does not encourage social work in a business setting. While limited success has been obtained in France, using subsidies, and in the United Kingdom, where the government has paid a stipend, these opportunities are ordinarily short term. Similarly, in New York City the privately based New York Partnership has successfully launched a summer jobs program for disadvantaged youth. But if countries seek to develop company-based OJT for large numbers of school leavers, they cannot be expected to focus on the disadvantaged. What is needed is a broad-based program to accommodate school leavers who decide to enter the world of business directly rather than pursuing advanced education.

This element of positively orienting a program for school leavers cannot be overemphasized. The contrast in the attitudes in Germany and France toward apprentices is striking. In Germany, apprentices are valued for their qualification obtained through three and a half years of arduous training. In France, apprentices are viewed disparagingly as those who could not continue their studies. A prerequisite to a successful program for school leavers is dignity and acceptance of this path as legitimate and respectable. The business community cannot be expected to be an instrument for coping with social misfits. Nor, incidentally, are those labeled as social misfits likely to be successful in business or other situations.

The value of OJT is increasingly recognized despite the dangers of the rigidities of traditional apprenticeship programs. Sweden provides an interesting case study of a country that abolished an extensive apprenticeship system and now seeks to introduce a greater emphasis on OJT.

Since 1955 the transfer of vocational education responsibilities from the apprenticeship system to the school system has been rapid. Eighty percent of all students in each cohort of about 100,000 now attend upper secondary school, with one-third taking the three- or four-year general track and the remaining two-thirds the two-year vocational track. A relatively small number of young persons are accommodated by company-based training. In 1975 approximately 5,000 students attended theoretical and practical training in companies. An additional 10,000 participated in attached training, in nursing, where it is most widespread, and in certain other selected occupational groups. This training was administered by the upper secondary school, with the company providing the theoretical and practical training. A small number of apprenticeships in the handicraft sector are supported by state grants. And some apprenticeships are included as part of total company training programs.

In a recent questionnaire sent to companies by the Swedish Employers' Confederation (SAF), great interest was expressed in expanding the role of companies in training. Almost 90 percent cited the need for greater latitude in retention and lower starting pay as important conditions to encourage more in-company training of young persons. A surprising 93 percent of the SAF companies thought apprenticeships were a good thing. Most SAF members have apprentices and would like to continue them in the future. Seventy-three percent of the companies considered apprenticeship training to be a very good alternative to existing vocational training. Many firms expressed a desire to see an increase in apprenticeships at the expense of other types of training. A recent SAF policy statement asserts: "Basic vocational training must be located more closely to business firms, especially the practical aspects of such training. . . . An educational place at school and training in the firm could be placed on an equal footing.[4]

In an address in February 1980, Bjorn Grünewald suggested a possible new direction:

The fact is that people agreed about transferring vocational training in particular from companies, as they were not able to provide a broad enough foundation, even in the practical elements of training. Even less could they manage the necessary general theoretical part. But now we have learned that the schools themselves cannot wholly manage to imitate reality behind closed doors. Perhaps the solution is to allow companies and schools each to contribute in positive interaction what each is best at.[5]

Indeed, the recently negotiated agreement to hire young workers for a six-month introduction may be the first step to a modernized apprenticeship program.

Broadly speaking, then, the lessons of Germany and Japan are that company-based OJT programs are attainable under the right circumstances. What remains to be determined is how to develop such a program in a country that does not have one. While the recent efforts of Sweden and the United Kingdom are noteworthy, countries attempting to enact such a program have met with great frustration, as described in Chapter 8.

NOTES

1. This section is based upon an interview with Mr. Friedberg, director of the training center for Dynamit Nobel, and the publication that describes their apprenticeship program.

2. This section benefited from interviews with a number of government and business officials. The system is described in Bundesandstalt fur Arbeit, *Employment Policy in Germany: Challenges and Concepts for the 1980s* (Nurnberg, Germany: Bundesandstalt fur Arbeit, 1980).

3. This section is based upon a number of interviews with government and business leaders. Officials at Tokyo Electric Power Company were particularly helpful. For an English-language treatment of the Japanese training system, *see* Toshio Ishikawa, *Vocational Training* (Tokyo: Japan Institute of Labor, 1981).

4. Swedish Employers' Confederation, *Preparation for a Future* (Stockholm: 1981), p. 11.

5. Bjorn Grünewald, *Creative School Makes Transition into Working Life Easier* (Stockholm: Swedish Employers' Confederation, February 1980), p. 13.

CHAPTER 6

Training and Job Creation

Among the alternatives to on-the-job training (OJT) that are sometimes suggested are job creation measures. Job creation has become a buzz-word in discussions about how to deal with unemployment and youth unemployment in particular. The connection is obvious. If, as we have argued, rising youth unemployment reflects in large part a diminution in the demand for labor, aren't job creation measures the most appropriate response? The logic is impeccable. All too often, however, advocates of particular programs play upon the ambiguity of the term *job creation* in a misleading way.

EDUCATION AND TRAINING

The expansion of schooling, upper secondary and postsecondary education in particular, has had major labor market impacts in the course of this century. As individuals attend school for longer and longer, they are removed from the regular labor market. As schooling is extended, the pool of full-time labor shrinks. In the United States, one effect of placing more and more young people in more and more education has been the virtual elimination of entry-level positions for those under 20.

American trade unions, as well as those in foreign countries, have recognized the impact of extending schooling in keeping large numbers of individuals from the labor markets. Thus, they have found it in the interests of their members to support increased education as a way of limiting labor supply. Japan, Sweden, France, and to a lesser extent the United Kingdom and Germany have all been affected by this trend since the 1960s. It helped them deal with the increase in young people entering the job market that occurred in the 1970s and 1980s.

Training positions also remove youth from the job market. The German apprenticeship program is the most dramatic example. Almost 50 percent of an age cohort is occupied in training for two to three years. CETA (Comprehensive Education and Training Act) programs have had a similar, though less dramatic effect. In fiscal 1980 over 3.6 million individuals participated in some program, and close to 2.2 million were under 22 years of age. An OECD report has credited CETA with reducing youth unemployment in the United States during the late 1970s.[1]

Sometimes it becomes difficult to distinguish training places from actual work. This is particularly true of training that is conducted in the work place. Perhaps the distinguishing characteristic of training places is that human resources investment is primary and social productivity secondary. Often individuals engaged in training will spend a portion of their time in the classroom, at public schools, company schools, or both. The trainees are ordinarily individuals starting out in the world of work. Since they are receiving valuable training they may receive less compensation than a full-time worker.

Sometimes, of course, training places may be misused by an employer who is eager to obtain cheap labor or who is unable to provide training because of lack of expertise or resources. In the German apprenticeship system, training places in bakeries and beauty salons have been criticized from this point of view. In response to the demand for more training places in the late 1970s, the number of places grew in these two types of establishments. It appears that small tradesmen in fact were willing to accept more apprentices because their productivity was quite high in relationship to their compensation. Since most of the placements are in small establishments, the training was mostly OJT. Clearly an effective system of training requires careful monitoring. The other side of the issue, however, is the need to structure the program in such a way that it does not place an unfair burden on businesses that are willing to undertake these training activities.

Training and education programs, then, have two primary effects. First, they remove individuals from the labor market. To the extent that they involve large numbers of individuals for an extended period of time, they can have dramatic effects on labor supply. Second, they provide advantages to trainees, particularly in OJT placements, in obtaining permanent positions. They do not by themselves create permanent positions in the labor market.

Such programs may, however, have secondary impacts on the productivity of companies and hence their growth. By providing trained personnel and a more rational recruitment process, they may help companies to become more effective, resulting in greater growth and more jobs. While such effects are to be hoped for, they are an added bonus and one that would be difficult to measure. Another side benefit of training programs may be to demonstrate the value of trained personnel. Once an employer has invested in training, he may be inclined to keep a trainee in a permanent position rather than hire a succession of workers. But such results are difficult to demonstrate.

One of the most successful American training programs under MDTA and CETA has been the Job Corps, which creates temporary training positions for disadvantaged youth. It provides a good case study of the job creation possibilities of training programs.

JOB CORPS

One of the legacies of the New Deal was the "make-work" project to provide government-funded jobs for those faced with unemployment. These make-work projects, which provide wages instead of welfare or unemployment checks, have two beneficial social effects: society is improved; and the money these people receive and spend has a pump-priming effect on the economy as a whole. In addition, the esteem of the participants is increased as well as their income.

When the social theorists of the Great Society decided to do something about unemployment, they borrowed this new concept of "make-work." Two "make-work" projects established under the Economic Opportunity Act of 1964 for youth that have continued to the present are the Job Corps and the Summer Youth Jobs Program. While encountering many difficulties when they initially began, these programs have come to be accepted by Congress as basically worthwhile and are consistently renewed. They are once again contained in the Jobs Training Partnership Act of 1982.

The Job Corps, perhaps more than any other portion of CETA, was continually and widely cited as a program success.[2] It is targeted on the disadvantaged and has maintained an admirable record in this regard. A review of participants in the spring of 1977 indicated that over 75 percent came from minority backgrounds. Between 85 and 90 percent of the corps members had not completed high school at the time they enrolled. Almost all corps members had experienced poverty. Many had been rejected from the armed forces, and close to 40 percent had been arrested.

But not only has the Job Corps been successfully targeted on disadvantaged youth, it has also been administered well and achieved results. The program consists of remedial education, vocational training, health care, and counseling in a residential setting.

Job Corps centers are either operated by private contractors selected through competitive bidding and known as contract centers or operated by the Department of Agriculture or the Department of the Interior on public land, and referred to as civilian conservation centers (CCCs), alluding to their similiarity to the famous Civilian Conservation Corps (CCC) of the New Deal.

Although established by the Economic Opportunity Act of 1964, since

1970 the Job Corps has been administered by the Department of Labor. Starting out as a small program, by 1973 it had served 184,800 individuals. It is an intensive program, for the most part in residential settings, combining basic literacy and numeracy instruction with skill training. The vocational fields covered include clerical, culinary arts, construction, automotive mechanics, and health. Participants receive a subsistence wage.

Under the Youth Employment Demonstration Projects Act (YEDPA) the program was doubled in size, eventually including more than 100 Job Corps centers with a capacity of over 48,000 young people. Of the 46,200 leavers for whom reports were made, 34,700 were available for placement, out of which 90 percent were placed in employment, military service, school, or further training. Considering the background of Job Corps participants, the record that has been developed is very impressive.

A recent series of evaluations of the Job Corps indicates that it is moderately successful in increasing employment and earnings, improving future labor market opportunities and reducing dependence and criminality. For 1977, with 40,000 youths enrolled, it was estimated that the social benefit totaled approximately $90 million, 60 percent attributed to the value of the output produced and 30 percent to a reduction in criminal activity among the corpsmen. This resulted in a net gain of $2,300 per corpsman.

A program similar to the Job Corps has developed in the United Kingdom to provide jobs for the disadvantaged under the auspices of the Manpower Services Commission. In October 1975, a variety of job creation schemes were introduced, resulting in over 58,000 jobs by the end of 1976. Initially most projects were sponsored by local authorities, but voluntary bodies and community groups have increasingly become involved. During 1981, as part of the Youth Opportunities Program, over 42,000 placements were made in community service and training workshop projects that have developed out of those job creation schemes.[3] The new name more accurately reflects the fact that individuals, many of whom are young, receive subsistence employment as they produce socially useful work, often improving the environment of the community. This program, like the Job Corps, has been quite successful in mounting socially useful projects and helping the disadvantaged. Many of the projects are run by locally organized community groups.

These programs are in some respects similar to programs of national service, such as the Peace Corps and Vista, as well as the military service. The military has also from time to time engaged in programs explicitly aimed at training workers. They administered the Civilian Conservation Corps of the New Deal and during the War on Poverty administered a project aimed at providing job skills to the disadvantaged. Although the training components in some of these programs differ from that of the Job Corps, they are all similar in providing short-term alternatives to the existing labor market. Of course, in the case of the military, career options are available, removing an individual from the labor market for 20 or 30 years, and in some cases permanently.

Another program that has continued to receive congressional reauthorization is the Summer Youth Employment Program, providing jobs to the disadvantaged. The results of this program are not as dramatic as those of the Job Corps. While its benefits of providing disadvantaged youth with jobs and income are well documented, its longer-term impact on participating youth has not been well documented. In fact its short duration, during summer vacation, makes it unlikely that its long-term impacts are substantial.

Programs involving temporary employment for youth at subsistence wages create jobs in the sense that they would not exist without specific government funding. But they are jobs for limited periods of time, providing subsistence wages and training. The longer-term success of such programs depends upon the availability of permanent placements in the labor market. A major reason for the Job Corps success is that it deals with a small group of individuals and an important emphasis is put on placement. Since the numbers are small, the impact on any local labor market is small. As such programs become larger and their impact on local labor markets becomes greater, their effectiveness will probably fall. It is one thing to integrate a small number of disadvantaged youth into an existing labor market. It is another to try to alter the character of the local labor market by promoting a significant percentage of those at the bottom of the job queue into jobs.

These programs can be more properly characterized, then, as temporary residential training programs, which to a large extent use OJT. They create training places, or what may be referred to as "youth jobs" for a limited number of individuals and help those youth enter the regular labor markets after a period of time. But they are not intended to create permanent jobs, expanding existing labor markets.

PUBLIC SERVICE EMPLOYMENT

So far I have described temporary job creation measures directed at young people entering the labor market. They are "learning jobs" in which inexperienced workers receive subsistence wages and training, often in a work setting. The Emergency Employment Act of 1971, which subsequently became Title IIB of CETA, had a different intent. In the midst of rising unemployment, Congress decided to provide money from the federal treasury to fund temporary jobs in state and local government. Between August 1971 and June 1973, over 404,000 individuals were employed in these positions. Of this number, 113,000 youth received summer jobs. In addition, 22 percent of the remaining positions went to those under 22. As unemployment stayed high, the pressure to maintain a program of public sector jobs resulted in Titles B and C in the CETA legislation of 1973, providing funds for placing workers in state and local positions. But as soon as these positions began to be filled, a paradox became apparent. State and local governments were being forced to lay off regular workers at the same time CETA envisioned them hiring the disadvantaged at lower salaries. The potential loss of efficiency and the obvious hostility that would be aroused led to a series of measures to allow state and local governments to retain incumbent workers. The unions, too, objected that new jobs should not be created to undercut existing wage scales.

While a quick end to the program might have cut short criticism, its extension in the Emergency Jobs Programs Extension Act of 1976 led to a far-reaching debate in Congress. Provisions were then made to ensure that Public Service Employment (PSE) projects would fund jobs only for low-income individuals who were long-term unemployed and would avoid substitution effects. It was not until the reauthorization of 1978, however, that legislative language effectuating these goals was adopted. Meanwhile, the damage that had already been done to PSE's reputation was substantial.[4]

The 1978 amendments lowered the pay levels of PSE jobs and mandated that they be reserved for low-income, long-term unemployed and for welfare recipients. A portion of the monies were reserved for training and employability counseling, and job length was limited to 18 months. Administrative measures to monitor compliance were strengthened by the establishment of an Office of Management Assistance, independent monitoring units (IMUs) at the local level, rigorous procedures for verifying the eligibility of applicants, and prime sponsor liability for program abuses.

However, despite the stated goal of improving placement into regular, full-time positions, job entry rates were lower in 1980 than in 1978. This resulted in part from worsening economic conditions and in part from success in targeting the program to the more disadvantaged. The basic underlying problem with PSE from its inception, since job placements were in the public sector, was that future jobs tended also to be in the public sector.

PSE seemed designed to raise controversy and produce failure. From the beginning its target population was ill defined, as was its strategy. Taken at face value it was a temporary job creation measure. It surely would have been more successful in this respect if it had used the "make-work" strategy of the New Deal in creating new jobs apart from existing institutions. The state and local governments, which had first welcomed the opportunity to employ more workers, failed to foresee the conflict between those they were laying off and those they were hiring. If PSE had been launched in prosperous times or at least when state and local governments were not cutting back programs, it might have avoided that problem. What state and local governments really wanted was authorization to use federal money to help retain workers on a temporary basis until they once again could pick up the costs. In retrospect this might have been a more successful approach. The CETA connection, with its emphasis on the disadvantaged, created conflict and confused the issues. In fact what was needed was a measure to help the unemployed, regardless of whether they were disadvantaged. The semantic controversy over what constituted "disadvantaged" only reinforced the anger of the unemployed persons caught in such a dispute. Such a result in times of large-scale unemployment is, of course, predictable.

The purpose of PSE was both humane and understandable. In a time of increasing unemployment, its intent was to put back to work large numbers of unemployed individuals. As a temporary job creation measure it might have succeeded. But as it became evident that the economy was not turning around, it was extended without any plausible strategy for success. Pressures arose to keep individuals already employed in their jobs, despite limitations in the statute. These individuals had nowhere to go, while others sought their places. As unemployment continued to be widespread, workers who were losing their jobs sought CETA employment, too. The temporary jobs strategy did not have long-term viability. When that finally became clear, the program was eliminated, as had the Swedish temporary jobs program for youth.

PSE's legacy was to undermine the political viability of large-scale temporary job creation by labeling it a failure. When in 1978 it was refocused on the disadvantaged and limited to 18 months, it began to look like the more traditional CETA training programs. But if PSE was intended as a training program to lead to eventual jobs, what was the sense of providing public sector placements, which would make it more difficult to obtain private sector jobs? PSE was shot through with contradictions, from its inception. It encompassed too many high hopes without a viable strategy for their attainment.

When the new Republican administration, elected in 1980, decided to phase out PSE, even its former supporters did not object. The conflict it generated and its failures indicated once more the inadequacies of government programs with good intentions but no strategy for success. The Jobs Training Partnership Act of 1982 eliminated PSE, but the dilemma it sought to resolve remained: How could government effectively move to provide jobs in times of high unemployment? In fact, the midterm election of 1982 indicated such widespread concern with unemployment that a special session of Congress with presidential backing in an apparent resurrection of the PSE approach passed a measure to create construction jobs financed through a new gasoline tax.

CREATING PRIVATE SECTOR JOBS

While the difficulties of public sector job creation have been generally recognized, private sector job creation is still favored by many. It is continually asserted that private sector OJT programs create "jobs." But the analysis that was applied to public sector OJT is equally applicable. An OJT training place is a temporary slot, which must then be converted to a permanent job. From the point of view of the individual it may look like a job has been created, but at the end of the training program the individual must seek regular employment. If the training place results in employment with the same employer, the job ordinarily is one that has always existed and might have gone to someone else.

One appealing aspect of private sector training is that the costs may be assumed by the employer at a considerable saving to the government. In fact, in both Germany and Japan the costs of OJT are absorbed by the employers. The result is a greatly reduced burden on general tax revenues. This aspect of private sector training makes it appealing but does not itself result in job creation.

The situation is further confused by the policy ambiguity that sometimes treats training places like jobs. For example, CETA monies were used to fund new positions that did not exist before and in which the individual received little training. The salary was often comparable to what a regular worker would receive. If that position were kept in force after the CETA funding expired it would look as if a job had been created. Of course, it might also be asserted that such a situation flies in the face of the intent of CETA, since it did not provide training. In fact, however, it is often difficult to say how much training is provided in OJT situations. So that what to one person may appear to be a training place, to another is a job, with only minimal training. Where the individual hired under CETA is hired permanently, the tendency would be to interpret the "training" provision loosely.

There are other instances where the government explicitly subsidizes the hiring of an individual in the hope that that individual may subsequently be incorporated into the work force. This might be considered the paradigm of successful job creation. The problem, of course, becomes trying to determine when in fact the subsidy actually creates a new job. What is known as substitution is in fact much more likely. Substitution refers to the situation where an individual who is hired replaces another individual who was working or might have been hired. In this situation, the job creation measure has resulted in the substitution of a particular individual, the one for whom a subsidy was received, for another individual, who might have otherwise been hired. While from the individual's point of view that may appear to be job creation, from society's point of view it is merely substitution of one individual for another.

In the case of real job creation, a company because of a subsidy hires a worker and then is able to expand its work force because of increasing production and resulting expansion, which would not have occurred in the absence of the subsidy. In certain situations a business might not hire workers at subsidized wages, but it would be an unusual situation. By far the greater tendency would be for companies contemplating expansion to take advantage of the subsidy. It would be virtually impossible to prevent all companies that were contemplating expansion to hire subsidized workers instead of workers at regular wages. The major impact of such a program would be to lower the costs of hiring new workers, in fact subsidizing such efforts, across the board. The expense of such a program might be considerable, as might the ensuing distortion caused by linking new expansion to hiring new workers and meddling in existing labor markets. It might also result in adverse effects upon the hiring of older workers.

The Targeted Jobs Tax Credit authorized by the Revenue Act of 1978 is an example of such a job creation program. It allows employers who hire certain targeted groups to benefit from a tax credit for a portion of the wages paid. By September 30, 1980, 139,000 young people aged 16 to 18 were hired under cooperative education programs and an additional 114,000 disadvantaged were hired, about one-fifth of whom were under 22. This program acts much like OJT, by providing a subsidy for a limited time for hiring these workers, except that no training is required. At least one analyst has argued that such programs can provide general economic stimulus when the jobs created are new ones.[5] The credit may stimulate employment, decrease the hours worked by individuals, and reduce prices. However, another commentator has suggested that it would be preferable to use the tax credit approach to encourage training of new workers.[6]

The Western European countries have used private sector job creation sparingly. The Swedish Work Relief Program, which was described in Chapter 3, was established in the aftermath of the 1973–1974 recession, when it was believed that the job shortfall would be temporary. That program was designed for those between 16 and 21 who were unemployed and provided private sector as well as public sector jobs subsidized at 75 percent. By providing large numbers of jobs to young people, however, many were being encouraged to leave school for the higher pay. It became clear that overall costs could be reduced by sending the same young people to school. The program became unpopular and was discontinued.

A special program begun in July 1981 by the Conservative government in the United Kingdom is of particular note. The Young Workers' Scheme provided government subsidies for all young persons hired at 45 pounds or less per week. The company received a subsidy of 7.5 pounds for all those hired at a weekly salary between 40 and 45 pounds and a subsidy of 15 pounds for all those who received 40 pounds or less. While sometimes described as a job creation program, its actual purpose was to reduce the wage paid to young workers. Its cost was substantial, since all those who hired workers for the first time were eligible for the subsidy. In fact, its implementation was impeded by the European Economic Community, which thought it might be an unfair attempt to manipulate labor costs. But its job creation effects have not been demonstrated.

Several French measures, including the waiver of social security tax for hiring young workers and the subsidy for entering into employment contracts with young workers, are sometimes labeled job creation measures. But their primary effect is to provide benefits to the young in promoting their place in the job queue. An authoritative evaluation of these programs is candid in admitting that the chief effect of these programs has been reducing unemployment directly by taking the program participants out of the labor market, rather than stimulating long-range employment of these individuals.[7] The evaluation goes on to argue the more tenuous point that the subsidy helped expand employment by reducing the costs of labor relative to capital and that adult employment was not affected.

The Work Creation Schemes (WCS) in Germany are part of a carefully thought out overall labor market strategy administered by the Budesanstalt fur Arbeit.[8] In recent years there has been an effort to foster private sector employment, focusing on workers who have been hard to employ, rather than young persons, who are instead referred to training places. In May 1979, the federal government launched a major program known as the "500 Million Deutsche Mark Program" to stimulate employment in regions with special employment problems. The program consisted of vocational training of employees in firms facing serious problems in adjusting to economic and technological change, reintegration of unskilled and long-term unemployed, and public employer subsidies for public works creation. Even with a relatively generous subsidy, the impact on permanent hiring of hard-core unemployed was small. This confirmed early studies of the more general hiring subsidy that had been in effect since 1969. The explanation given is that wage costs are not always the factor discouraging hiring of disadvantaged workers. A mixture of skill deficits, lack of self-confidence, unstable work habits or attitudes, and a "superficial stigma" (such as ethnicity, religion, sex, or criminal record) are much greater and need to be addressed directly. The study author suggests that a more extensive employment effort not targeted as narrowly would have greater stimulative effect by returning the wage costs to the local economy and thus stimulating aggregate demand.

By and large, then, these private sector subsidy programs, which are not training programs, are ways of providing movement on the job queue for workers in a disadvantaged position. Subsidies create substitution effects. They substitute the subsidized workers for workers who would have been taken on without subsidy. While it is conceivable that in some cases the decision to hire would not have been made in the absence of the subsidy, this would have to be demonstrated. In existing evaluations the substitution effects seem to outweigh strongly the stimulative effect on new hires, despite theoretical arguments.[9]

Indeed, the central factor in private sector hiring undoubtedly is current and future needs for additional labor. Unless an employer is expanding, it will not consider employing additional personnel. As we have already seen, one of the difficulties of job creation schemes is that they are often developed in times of recession, when most companies are cutting back rather than expanding. But if a company is interested in hiring new employees, its decision would be based upon the cost of new workers as compared to their expected productivity. In order for these job creation schemes to be successful, then, they must operate within the arena of decision where they make the difference between a decision not to hire and a decision to hire. If a company can purchase labor on the existing labor market and make a profit by additional production, the job creation schemes are not necessary. The schemes will only be successful where the labor subsidy to the company enables the company to anticipate a profit, while under ordinary market conditions a profit could not be anticipated. Of course, the power of government subsidy may be considerably enhanced, since many such decisions are made under conditions of risk. Companies may view the risk differently if the start-up cost to them is reduced.

Where such a program actually creates jobs that have not previously existed, its adverse effects upon other workers may be considered minimal. However, one of the difficulties of creating such a program is to limit it to only those companies that would otherwise not have hired. Actual evaluations indicate varying success in achieving such targeting. As a result for each new job created, many more jobs that would have been created in any case will be subsidized. The result is that the costs of the programs may be quite high in relationship to the benefit of new jobs created. Also, the substitution effects may adversely affect other groups competing with the favored group. Thus older workers may find themselves at a disadvantage. Or other young workers may find they lose out to subsidized young workers. This may have unhealthy political effects by pitting one group of needy individuals against another.

Another factor increasing the costs of such programs is the high cost of compliance with government regulations. Paperwork costs may be significant, as well as liaison costs. As the government attempts to ensure that the quality of jobs is at a certain level and that training of a certain level is provided, the costs of complying and demonstrating compliance may be considerable.

Another possible adverse effect of such subsidies might be to increase the costs to the employer if the subsidies in fact deter the employer from the rational decision in an attempt to take advantage of the subsidy. Also, the subsidies have the effect of providing benefits to particular firms that might work against overall productivity.

In general, private sector subsidies have neither been used on a large scale nor been overly successful. They would appear to be most advisable as part of an across-the-board economic development strategy. Under conditions of relatively high employment, they might also be used to stimulate regional economic development. In times of high unemployment, targeted subsidies are more likely to channel what little hiring is going on into specified channels. It is imperative in such situations that these subsidies are being used to accomplish some overarching social good. Otherwise they are unfair and merely provide side payments to employers for doing what they would do in any case—a poor use for public funds, particularly when they are in short supply.

Both public and private sector job schemes have been oversold. In part this reflects the wishful thinking of lawmakers and others who are looking for quick fixes to economic ills. In part it reflects a confusion about program objectives and program impacts. Aside from the philosophical difficulties of justifying job creation programs for the young, when unemployment is generally high it is likely that targeted subsidies will result in substantial substitution effects, thus hurting other groups. Real job creation makes much more sense, linked to carefully thought out macroeconomic policies to achieve overall economic growth in the economy. But the usefulness of training and education places as a way of removing individuals from the labor market remains an important and potent incentive especially in times of job scarcity.

NOTES

1. *Youth Without Work* (Paris: OECD, 1981), p. 208.

2. Mathematica Policy Research, *Evaluation of the Economic Impact of the Job Corps Program, Second Follow-up Report* (Princeton, N.J.: Mathematica Policy Research, 1980). Material from this report is cited in the following pages.

3. Manpower Services Commission *Youth Task Group Report* (London: MSC, April 1982), Annex 3.

4. William Mirengoff et al., *CETA: Accomplishments, Problems, Solutions* (Washington, D.C.: Bureau of Social Science Research, 1981).

5. Jeffrey Perloff and Michael Wachter, "The New Jobs Tax Credit: An Evaluation of the 1977–78 Wage Subsidy Program," *American Economic Review*, 69 (1979): 173–179.

6. David Robinson, "Youth Access to Private Sector Jobs: The Sorcerer's Apprentice," in U.S. Vice President's Task Force on Youth Employment *A Review of Youth Employment Problems, Programs and Policies*, vol. 3 (Washington, D.C.: Government Printing Office, 1980).

7. Frederique Pate et al., "Les Pactes Nationaux pour l'Emploi des Jeunes," *Travail et emploi*, no. 6 (1980): 23–26.

8. Bundesanstalt fur Arbeit, *Employment Policy in Germany: Challenges and Concepts for the 1980s* (Nurnberg, Germany: Bundesanstalt fur Arbeit, 1980).

9. Joseph Ball et al., *The Participation of Private Businesses as Work Sponsors in the Youth Entitlement Demonstration* (New York: Manpower Demonstration Research Corporation, 1981).

CHAPTER 7

Comprehensive Youth Initiatives

Many of the programs adopted in the United States and abroad to combat youth unemployment have been directed at specific groups such as the disadvantaged and minorities. Others have attempted to affect broader classes of individuals. The Smith-Hughes Act of 1917 is an example of a broad-based program to provide secondary school students with skills necessary to obtain jobs. The German apprenticeship program is even broader in focus, providing on-the-job training (OJT) for almost all secondary school leavers.

Both of these programs also have secondary labor market effects since they remove large numbers of youth from the labor market for the period that they are engaged in training. In this sense the systematic rise in the age for compulsory education and the encouragement of longer years of schooling may be seen as labor market strategies much cheaper than providing subsidized jobs. Similarly, compulsory national service, whether in military or civilian programs, removes many young persons from the job market and in addition may provide skill training to young people.

As the levels of youth unemployment, particularly among those 16, 17, and 18, have continued to rise since the mid–1970s, longer-range, comprehensive solutions have been sought. Recently the idea of a youth guarantee has taken hold in the Scandinavian countries and in the European Economic Community. This is a commitment to provide all young people with education, training, or a job. Of the countries in this study, Sweden, the United Kingdom, and France have all committed themselves in one form or another to that concept.

But before considering these relatively recent developments, I will look at an earlier effort undertaken in the United States, the Youth Employment Demonstration Projects Act, a series of measures designed to implement a youth employment policy.

THE YOUTH EMPLOYMENT DEMONSTRATION
PROJECTS ACT

In 1977, the U.S. Congress enacted the Youth Employment Demonstration Projects Act (YEDPA) to combat rising youth unemployment.[1] Responding to the popularly expressed feeling that the rate of youth unemployment, particularly among the poor and minorities, was unacceptably high, Congress adopted a wide-ranging solution. Most congressmen were not aware of the subtleties of calculating unemployment rates. Nor did they know why this particular legislation should succeed when its predecessors had not. Yet, despite YEDPA's ambiguous results, if Jimmy Carter had been reelected president, the successor to YEDPA, the Youth Act of 1980, at an estimated cost of $3.7 billion for fiscal 1981, would most probably have become law.

But the Youth Act of 1980 was caught up in the election of 1980 and was deferred to the following spring. By then Ronald Reagan had been elected president, and it was deader than a doornail. In fact, it was so dead that much of the research into its impact was stopped in its tracks by an administration seemingly intent on getting out of the business of youth training and employment as quickly as possible.

YEDPA is notable, however, for having mobilized resources toward solving the problem of youth unemployment and having pointed toward a comprehensive policy regarding youth employment, even though it did not articulate one definitive approach. Instead, in perhaps the most ambitious attempt at social experimentation since the Office of Economic Opportunity (OEO) was established in 1964, YEDPA set out to establish, field test, and evaluate new approaches to employing youth.

YEDPA passed Congress in 1977 as a little-noted amendment to the existing Comprehensive Employment and Training Act (CETA). Once in place it gathered increasing popularity among legislators and looked headed for permanence in the Carter administration's Youth Act of 1980. But some legislative difficulties, in part associated with the vagaries of an election year, and the victory of President Ronald Reagan cut short a popular, if somewhat difficult to categorize, example of social experimentation.

In one sense YEDPA refocused, embellished, and regrouped a number of existing programs—a cosmetic attempt to demonstrate that the problem of youth unemployment justified a special and coordinated response. Table 7.1 indicates how YEDPA built upon existing CETA programs.

YEDPA called for expenditures of close to $2 billion for fiscal 1978, roughly double the amount allocated in fiscal 1977 for youth-oriented programs under CETA. Approximately $700 million went to the Sum-

Table 7.1
A Comparison of Federal Youth Programs Based Upon Fiscal Years 1977
and 1978
(in millions of dollars)

Outlays Prior to YEDPA		Outlays Under YEDPA	
CETA Summer	575	Summer Youth Employment Program	700
Youth Conservation Corps	48	Job Corps	234
Job Corps, CETA Title IV	202	Youth Incentive Entitlement Pilot Projects	115
High School Work Study	10	Youth Employment and Training Programs	403
Federal Summer Aide	35	Youth Adults Conservation Corps	233
Stay-in-School	66	Youth Community Conservation and Improvement Projects	115
Federal Summer Employment	20	Demonstrations	110
Totals	956		1,910

Source: Adapted from Andrew Hahn, "Taking Stock of YEDPA," *Youth and Society* 2, no. 2 (December 1979): 248, 249.

mer Youth Employment Programs (SYEP), a modest increase over the fiscal 1977 allocation. The Job Corps was slightly expanded, although by fiscal 1980 it more than doubled in size from fiscal 1977. Another area of increased funding resulted from the creation of two new community conservation programs building upon the experience of the Youth Conservation Corps.

The major new departures of YEDPA were the Youth Incentive Entitlement Pilot Projects (YIEPP), the Youth Employment and Training Program (YETP), and some special demonstration projects funded through discretionary funds given to the secretary of labor. YIEPP was designed to help economically disadvantaged youth complete high school, in a program reminiscent of the Neighborhood Youth Corps. Youths in 17 impacted geographic areas between the ages of 16 and 19 from households that were beneath the poverty level or received welfare were provided guaranteed year-round jobs (part-time during the school year and full-time during the summer) if they agreed to attend high school, return to school, or enroll in an equivalency program. YETP sought to enhance the job prospects and career preparation of low-income youth between the ages of 14 through 21 through a range of services, including basic education, information about the labor market, apprenticeship, institutional training, and on-the-job training.

YEDPA also created a special Office of Youth Programs within the Employment and Training Administration of the Department of Labor, which coordinated formula grant programs, special discretionary demonstrations, technical assistance, and research and evaluation. The discretionary activity funded under YEDPA for basic research, national demonstration projects, and assessment activities involved more than twice the federal dollars spent for research on the War on Poverty. Between January 1978 and spring 1979, 2.5 million youth, which represented 6.9 percent of all youth, reported involvement in some CETA youth program. The impact on black youth was particularly profound. In 1978, 44 percent of black youth aged 14 to 19 who held a job had been enrolled in a federal employment program.

The systematic approach to planning and evaluating in YEDPA was impressive, and the findings of its research are important, if not surprising. The programs were generally successful in reaching disadvantaged minority youth, even if some problems did arise. The Youth Community Conservation and Improvement Projects (YCCIP) and the Job Corps, for example, were not successful in reaching women. The work experiences provided by these programs were dominated by clerical, maintenance, and recreational jobs. In a survey of YETP, YCCIP, and the SYEP work sites, it was found that approximately one-third of the sites consisted of general maintenance work and 20 percent clerical work.[2] In the entitlement program, YIEPP, through 1979, 27 percent were placed in clerical positions, 26 percent in building or maintenance, and 15 percent as community workers and recreational aides. While these jobs were for the most part positive work experiences, they did not provide entrance into career positions.

YEDPA proved that large-scale job creation for youth in the public sector can be accomplished rapidly and that over time the quality of these placements will improve markedly. But the program impacts were not overwhelmingly favorable. While all programs resulted in increased hourly wages for those leaving them, it is not clear that these results can be attributed to the programs themselves. Nor is it clear that these effects would have continued in future years.

The placement rates for YETP of one in four and for YCCIP of one in five indicate that both programs for in-school youth and out-of-school youth were not very successful in placing youth in real jobs. Their contrast with the Job Corps placement rate of 68 percent for fiscal 1978 is revealing. The Job Corps, of course, is a well-established program of more narrow and focused scope.

When these placement rates are measured against the substantial costs of these programs, their efficiency becomes questionable. The Congressional Budget Office estimated the cost of serving one participant for an entire year in YIEPP as $9,550, in YETP as $5,307, and YIEPP as $4,596. While the results of these programs in terms of encouraging youth to remain in school and attain work experience may be admirable, their cost is hardly justified in terms of their placement record. In fact, YEDPA was really not designed to produce permanent jobs. By and large it followed previous models in relying upon public sector placements and emphasizing training places rather than permanent jobs. The emphasis on staying in school focused attention away from the placement aspects by interposing a separate criterion of program success.

YEDPA's lack of concrete achievements made it vulnerable, despite congressional support for this youth-oriented program. In the budget-cutting mood reinforced by President Reagan's substantial electoral majority, most of these youth programs were eliminated. The major survivors are the two programs initiated by the Economic Opportunity Act of 1964, which had developed a loyal congressional constituency: the Job Corps and SYEP. Indeed, the Job Corps remained as the one training program for youth with a substantial success rate in placement. Perhaps the greatest loss in YEDPA was the failure to benefit from the lessons that it was so well designed to provide. In the haste to dismantle the program, many of the research findings were lost, and the quest for some overall solution to youth unemployment was abandoned.

THE SCANDINAVIAN YOUTH GUARANTEE

While YEDPA was phased out and forgotten by the Reagan administration, the idea of a comprehensive approach to youth unemployment is alive in Scandinavia.[3] No other group of countries has been so concerned with addressing the youth employment problem, in spite of the fact that their rates of youth unemployment have been relatively small when compared to other Western European countries. A recent report of the Nordic Council concluded that the results of existing initiatives to combat youth unemployment had been far from sufficient. While these measures have had a positive effect in helping individuals qualify for jobs, no positive trend in reduction of youth unemployment has developed. These measures, it was concluded, had been insufficient in scope.

The steering group preparing the report found that in all Nordic Council countries support for a youth guarantee was strong among both the political parties and the parliaments. The steering group endorsed the approach of a youth guarantee but noted that the details of its implementation in each country needed to be worked out. While the youth guarantee would involve some combination of jobs, training, and schooling for all youth within a certain age group, the exact nature of the guarantee would have to be decided upon in each country.

The report cites a variety of measures adopted by individual members of the Nordic Council to deal with youth unemployment. Finland instituted temporary vocational courses for 16 and 17 year olds, guidance courses, further vocational training places, favorable study grants, and an additional tenth year of schooling. Other measures included subsidies to companies and municipalities for entering apprenticeship contracts with the young, subsidies for hiring young people at contractual wages, and direct hiring by the state of a limited number of those who have completed vocational education or advanced training.

In Denmark a series of measures have been directed at all those unemployed under 25, but emphasizing the "residuary group." These measures include: 10- to 12-week courses for the unemployed to provide motivation and labor market information, subsidization to public and private sector employers for providing jobs that include training at contractual wages, employment projects organized by counties and municipalities to employ youth at 80 percent of contractual wages, and finally, subsidized private sector jobs lasting 6 to 12 months for youth.

Norway has adopted education and labor market strategies for those under 20. They include vocationally oriented programs for those under 20 for up to 8 weeks, subsidized training by private companies for up to 13 weeks, admission in some instances for 18 and 19 year olds into vocational courses for those over 20, subsidies to private employers to place those under 19 on subsidized jobs for not more than 13 weeks at contractual wages, special jobs in municipal, county, and state administrations, and special work experience projects for young persons with special problems lasting from 3 to 6 months.

Sweden has adopted vocational training similar to that in other Scandinavian countries: short vocational guidance courses within the school system; special provisions for young persons to participate in vocational courses for those over 20, including a stipend; subsidized state and municipal hiring at contractual wages; subsidized private sector jobs for up to six months; and special projects, including alternate periods of theoretical and practical training. While prior to 1980 an active labor market policy had resulted in hiring over 50,000 young persons in public employment, in the summer of 1980 the government shifted responsibility for 16 and 17 year olds to the education authorities.

Turning the matter over to secondary school authorities has not, however, solved it. Despite efforts to expand the secondary school, a substantial number of youngsters do not remain and are seeking alternatives. With the demise of the work relief program, a program of vocational introduction was developed in which young people under the age of 18 could be offered work experience in a company for up to 40 weeks. They received a stipend similar to that of those attending upper secondary school. While many business leaders praised this program, it was opposed by the trade unions as providing a source of cheap labor.

A new program of jobs for the young has been introduced by mutual agreement between the Swedish Employers' Confederation (SAF) and the Confederation of Swedish Trade Unions (LO) and the Central Organization of Salaried Employees (PTK). Jobs for the young will be provided by business firms whenever the employer and the unions are agreed that this can be done. They are intended for 16 and 17 year olds who would not otherwise obtain places at high school or ordinary jobs. They will be employed for a specific period of time not to exceed six months. Both the companies and unions accept responsibility to ensure that the young people are given meaningful and developing work. As soon as suitable training or suitable ordinary work is offered, they shall leave. While they are working they receive 85 Swedish kroner per day. The employer is reimbursed 75 Swedish kroner per day and must in addition assume the social security charges. Where possible and appropriate, training is arranged in conjunction with the schools and labor exchanges.

This program of jobs for the young could very well form the basis for an OJT training program in firms that would cater to those leaving secondary school. The progression from the work relief program to a vocational introduction to the present jobs for the young may be viewed as the development of a middle road. From the employers' point of view it provides them with an opportunity to introduce young people to the world of work and select successful youngsters to continue on in the firm. From the union perspective it provides controls over a program for the young which ensures that they will not become a source of alternative cheap labor threatening the positions of their members. From society's point of view a program has been developed to provide an alternative to 17 and 18 year olds who leave school that points them in a productive direction and helps them make the transition to working life. With a greater emphasis on training and a longer duration, such a program could go a long way to making the youth guarantee a reality.

YOUTH GUARANTEE BRITISH STYLE

Talk of the youth guarantee, as mentioned earlier, has penetrated the European Economic Community. In *A New Training Initiative* proposed by the Manpower Services Commission (MSC) of the United Kingdom in December 1981 it was asserted "that for the first time there is agreement amongst employers, unions, the education and training services and other interests that *all* young people entering employment need good quality basic training as a foundation for work." The commission favored "as rapid steps as possible . . . to establish vocational preparation arrangements covering *all* young people entering the labour market."[4] The progression in the United Kingdom has been dramatic from a program aimed at hard-to-employ youth to a program aimed at all youth. The progression has reflected the mammoth increase in youth unemployment, covering all abilities.

While the United Kingdom is the country in our study with the least reliance on upper secondary school, the rising unemployment problem there among 16, 17, and 18 year olds has been the most drastic. In the absence of jobs and without a schooling option, large numbers have become unemployed. To make matters worse, the extensive apprenticeship system that not long ago provided placements for 40 percent of the boys in an age cohort has been diminishing rapidly. The need for an alternative system in the United Kingdom was greater than in any other country under study.

The major program to come to the aid of unemployed youth has been the Work Experience on Employer's Premises (WEEP) program. During 1981 over 240,000 youngsters obtained placements at a subsistence allowance of 25 pounds per week for an average length of 22 weeks. It was this program that the MSC proposed to expand in the document cited above. As a step in that direction, they proposed to involve the employers and trade unions in the development of the scheme. The result was the *Youth Task Group Report* of April 1982, which proposed a scheme ultimately to include all young people aged 16 and 17 who left full-time education. In a refreshing departure, rather than guaranteeing them schooling, the proposal will guarantee them the opportunity of entering training or a period of planned work experience combined with work-related training and education. Coverage is also anticipated for 18 year olds with special needs.

Acknowledging that sufficient public and private resources are not available immediately, the intent is to provide opportunities for all 16 year olds and all 17 year olds who become unemployed within the first year, by September 1983.

The participants will receive a subsistence wage, similar to that previously received under WEEP, of approximately 1,400 pounds per annum. The distinction will be in the greater effort made to provide high-quality training and to emphasize longer-term placements of one year or more. The plan emerges as part of an effort to provide greater levels of training to those entering the work force.

FRANCE, GERMANY, AND JAPAN

In France, Les Pactes Nationaux pour l'Emploi have included a variety of approaches but have been more limited than those of other countries and have not expanded to include the growing numbers of unemployed youth.[5] By remaining small they have been able to maintain good placement records. In addition, educational opportunities continue to expand. There has been no effort as in the United States, Sweden, or the United Kingdom to introduce large-scale programs of work experience or OJT. The new Socialist government in France, however, has discussed launching a major new program to provide alternative training for youth between the ages of 16 and 18.[6] While it would incorporate the principle of alternance between school and the work place and rely heavily on making changes in the schools, it was also projected that in 1982 100,000 training places will be offered.

Germany and Japan already have comprehensive systems in place. In Germany, secondary school leavers are absorbed through the formal apprenticeship, and in Japan they are hired by companies that provide OJT.

DOES THE UNITED STATES NEED A COMPREHENSIVE APPROACH?

American pragmatism resists comprehensive approaches. We are skeptical of "guarantees," whether to youth or otherwise, but the need to confront the situation of our youth anew should be evident. The Smith-Hughes Act of 1917 and the larger policy of the comprehensive high school served us well during the first half of the twentieth century. Since the mid–1960s, however, we have been confronted with a growing problem of youth unemployment. This problem has been exacerbated by economic recession, but it reflects long-term changes in the youth labor market. We need measures to improve the economy and to add jobs to the economy, but we need also to take a closer look at our youth, particularly those between the ages of 16 and 19 who are not attending full-time school or would prefer to be in the labor market.

During the early part of the century it was not uncommon for youngsters of 12 or 13 to be working full time in factories. Compulsory school attendance was a great advance. It took young people out of the work place and exploitative conditions and placed them in public schools, where they could learn and develop. In the United States we developed a system in which all young people were expected to complete high school, and the great majority did. Then in the post–World War II period we developed a universal approach to postsecondary education. The state of California was one of the leaders, proclaiming that all high school graduates could attend community college and then go on to the state college system. We have made four years of college a prerequisite for many of the career positions in our society. But in the process of bestowing more and more education on individuals we have lost sight of the connection between education and working life. The educational system must in large part be judged by its ability to help young people make the transition to working life.

Unfortunately, governments confronted with numbers of unemployed youth follow the easier path by encouraging them to remain in school. The schools are maintained by the government and subject to the wishes of government officials. It is relatively easy to increase the capacity of schools. Furthermore, at first glance the economics seem persuasive. It is far cheaper to support a student in school, where the student typically receives a small stipend or none at all, than to provide a job with a salary in addition to training. The problem is that maintaining youth in schools does not contribute to social productivity, nor does it necessarily enhance young people's work skills.

As a matter of educational and social policy, does it make sense to force individuals who want to work to extend their schooling? Is it wise to deprive students of an opportunity for work experience and contact with the adult world until after they have completed college? Does widespread use of college consign non-college graduates to second-class status in the labor market?

As we have required more and more students to attend school for longer and longer, the problem of transition has become greater. On the one hand, youth on the average remain in school longer before entering the world of work. But more importantly, as more schooling has become the norm, the labor market has adjusted so that career positions that once began at 14, 16, or 18 now begin in the mid-twenties. Consequently, those students leaving school at 16, 17, and 18 find that the best they can hope for is a temporary job in the secondary labor market with the prospect that in their mid-twenties they may find a career position providing the income necessary to lead a stable, adult life. Paradoxically, of course, these are the students most in need of help in making the transition to work but the ones who find themselves with the least guidance.

Given the high rates of unemployment, it seems unlikely that jobs will be available in the near future, but we can redouble our efforts in other directions. If we do not need a youth guarantee, we do need to provide youth with the opportunity to enter the world of work in a guided framework so they can continue their personal development and their socialization. We already have large numbers of students aged 16, 17, and 18 who are in comprehensive secondary school but would prefer to be working in the adult world. We also need to recognize that some young people who do complete secondary school but do not want to continue on to university immediately need the opportunity to gain practical work experience before continuing their schooling or pursuing a particular professional career.

The work opportunities that are currently available to youth are in the secondary labor market without career prospects. Since the work is temporary, the employer has little incentive to provide training. Yet, without training and job skills, the school leaver is destined to a life without a career.

Instead of scheming harder and harder to keep our young people in school longer and longer, we need to provide viable options. There is mounting evidence that large numbers of youngsters feel that formal schooling beyond 16 is neither necessary nor desirable. The problem of helping our young people make the transition to working life does not disappear if schooling is prolonged. In fact, the extension of schooling may indeed make the transition to working life harder than ever. Business leaders complain about the work attitudes of our young. Is it any wonder that individuals who have spent a large part of their lives in schools find it difficult to adjust to work?

Business leaders are well aware, in fact, that elaborate schemes for vocational education are not likely to increase the desirability of youth as employees. Given the rapid change in technology, companies are more interested in securing workers with basic literacy skills and good work habits than they are in obtaining workers with specialized training. But unfortunately, because the labor markets have been experiencing an oversupply, the tendency in many countries has been to defer hiring young workers. Business leaders have been slow to accept responsibility for participation in the training of workers at a younger age. Yet if companies are interested in having their workers better adapted to working conditions, what better way than to introduce young workers through training programs based in the company?

German and Japanese firms have continued to insist on hiring young workers and continue to provide in-company training programs. It is not accidental that the performance of these countries has been outstanding in the post–World War II era. The use of young workers and their introduction to the company at an early age provides important benefits to the company. These companies have clearly demonstrated that youth are not in need of more classroom training to perform more effectively on the job. While the Germans have developed highly effective three-and-a-half-year apprenticeship programs with formal curricula and considerable in-class instruction, the Japanese offer informal OJT based upon job rotation and the watchful guidance of senior workers.

Thus, in pursuing the short-term goals of expanding schooling, we are contributing to the perpetuation of the misleading myth that if only youth stay in school longer they will then find good jobs. What is needed instead is a strategy for developing new mechanisms for the transition of youth into the labor market with the emphasis on traineeships and the development of career positions.

While internship programs have multiplied for college graduates, traineeships for secondary school leavers have diminished. The ranks of secondary school leavers, whether graduates or not, is substantial, and these young people grow up maturing earlier than ever. But they find it harder and harder to enter into work situations that provide opportunities to develop their skills and their career prospects. As the informal career ladders break down, they have become the forsaken generation. They bounce from job to job in the secondary labor market.

Whether called a comprehensive solution or not, what is needed is an approach that recognizes a societal responsibility to 16, 17, and 18 year olds who do not continue on to college to provide work experiences that will provide them with the opportunities to develop careers. Given the movement of large corporations away from hiring youth and the likelihood that the supply of labor will be abundant for the foreseeable future, a major initiative is necessary. Unless something is done, the future promises lost generations of secondary school graduates and dropouts who are not integrated into productive roles in the American work force. To avoid this prospect, a cooperative program is needed involving government, business, and labor. Whether we can mount such an effort is, however, far from clear. I will turn now to an in-depth review of the history of government intervention and the response by employers and trade unions in order to assess our prospects for a viable youth unemployment policy.

NOTES

1. See the two excellent articles by Andrew Hahn, "Taking Stock of YEDPA," *Youth and Society* 2, no. 2 (December 1979): 237–261; and "Early Themes from YEDPA: The Federal Youth Employment Initiative—Part 2," 1980, mimeographed.

2. Joseph Ball et al., *The Participation of Private Businesses as Work Sponsors in the Youth Entitlement Demonstration* (New York: Manpower Demonstration Research Corporation, 1981).

3. Nordic Council of Ministers, *Youth Guarantee: Theory or Reality* (Secretariat of the Nordic Council of Ministers, June 1981).

4. Manpower Services Commission, *A New Training Initiative* (London: MSC, December 1981).

5. Frederique Pate et al., "Les Pactes Nationaux pour l'Emploi des Jeunes," *Travail et emploi*, no. 6 (1980): 15–62.

6. For an early version of the Socialist alternative, *see* Bertrand Schwartz, *L'Insertion professionnelle et sociale des jeunes: Rapport au premier ministre* (Paris: La Documentation Française, September 1981).

CHAPTER 8

The Limits of
Government Intervention

The advanced industrialized countries have adopted numerous measures, especially since the mid–1970s, to combat youth unemployment. The United States has led the way in volume and variety. While government efforts to alleviate youth unemployment began earlier in the United States, in the mid–1970s youth unemployment began soaring in Western Europe, and a similar concern for the problem developed. The United Kingdom, France, Germany, and Sweden, along with the other . Western European countries, adopted a variety of measures aimed at alleviating these problems. As might be expected, business and labor organizations, largely through their national confederations, have been interested and concerned with these matters.

Despite the fact that youth unemployment has been perceived by many as a critical problem in this country since the 1960s, there is still disagreement over whether it justifies governmental action. If government action is justified, should it be general measures to stimulate the economy and reduce overall unemployment or a specially targeted youth unemployment policy? A review of these various measures will poignantly demonstrate the limits of governmental intervention.

GOVERNMENT MEASURES

United States

When the Manpower Development and Training Act of 1962 (MDTA) was enacted, it incorporated ideas from the Areas Redevelopment Act of 1961, the Employment Act of 1946, and the GI Bill.[1] By the late 1960s it included a dozen categorical programs, each with its own appropriation account. The problem of coordinating this great variety of programs led to the adoption of the Comprehensive Employment and

Training Act of 1973 (CETA). Although CETA attempted to emphasize the involvement of the private sector in on-the-job training (OJT), the recession of 1974–1975 all but eliminated this effort. The interest of employers in hiring new workers flagged, and a massive program of public sector jobs was enacted, known eventually as Public Service Employment (PSE). These jobs were never meant to provide permanent employment. As government cutbacks continued in the early 1980s, those employed found it extremely difficult to move into full-time public sector jobs.

During 1977, the Youth Employment Demonstration Projects Act (YEDPA) was enacted. It consolidated such former youth employment programs as the Job Corps and the Summer Youth Employment Program. In addition, it created new demonstration projects aimed at keeping youth in school, providing out-of-school youth with jobs, and encouraging youth to return to school. For the most part these programs were designed to provide work experience in conjunction with schooling. While these work experiences were generally positive, they did not, by and large, provide a source of continued employment. YEDPA programs suffered the same difficulties in placing their participants as the CETA programs that had preceded them. When the Reagan administration came to power, the Carter-initiated Youth Act, which was to replace YEDPA, was dropped. PSE was phased out, and efforts were made to increase private sector involvement through the private industry councils (PICs) established in 1978. The Jobs Training Partnership Act of 1982 strengthened the PICs and minimized the use of stipends for trainees, focusing resources on actual training. In a separate action, a new tax was imposed on gasoline to fund a program of highway construction and produce new jobs.

Federal Republic of Germany

Germany has been quite successful in limiting youth unemployment, although more recently rates have increased markedly. The ratio of youth unemployment to general unemployment is also unusually low. In large part this must be attributed to the German system of vocational education, with its system of in-company apprenticeships, which provides large numbers of secondary school leavers and graduates with up to three and a half years of structural training and quasi-employment.

Prior to the general rise in youth unemployment, the Berufsbildungsgesetz of 1969 formalized and strengthened the system of apprenticeship under the Federal Vocational Training Institute.[2] Subsequently, the uniform curricula in the approximately 470 occupational categories were revised. Responding to the rising rates of youth unemployment in the mid–1970s, the Ausbildungsplatzforderungsgesetz

(Training Places Promotion Act) was passed in 1976. Unlike other Western European countries that passed a variety of measures to improve youth employment prospects, the German approach was able to draw upon a well-established program. The Training Places Promotion Act put pressure on employers to accept more trainees by threatening to institute a system of taxation to pay for additional training places if they were not voluntarily forthcoming. The number of volunteered training places increased, and this threatened tax was never imposed. More recently, new legislation has superseded the act of 1976 and abolished the threat of direct taxation.

Some other measures such as strengthened school-based vocational education have been undertaken. In certain skill areas, school-based programs have been substituted for on-the-job training. Several *Lander* (the equivalent of our states) have introduced experimental programs to provide a full year of vocational training before the OJT phase of the apprenticeship. Some *Lander* have also introduced a second day of in-school education to strengthen the theoretical basis of studies in the apprenticeship. A number of special programs have also been introduced to help the disadvantaged, which include both those with physical and mental disabilities and those who are culturally deprived, such as the children of foreign workers. While these programs have had some successes, they are overshadowed by the large-scale apprenticeship program.

United Kingdom

As in Germany, the school-leaving pattern in the United Kingdom has meant that large numbers of young people have entered the world of work after the age of 16. In fact, the United Kingdom explicitly emulated the German apprenticeship system so that during the early 1960s about 40 percent of 16 year old boys leaving school entered apprenticeships. However, unlike the German apprenticeship system, which was strengthened during the 1960s and 1970s, the United Kingdom apprenticeship system has been shrinking. By the 1980s the proportion of 16 year old boys entering the system was down to 20 percent, and apprenticeships declined from a peak of 236,000 in 1968 to under 150,000 in 1980 to about 100,000 in 1982.

Efforts in the United Kingdom instead have focused on increasing educational opportunities and special programs to provide supplementary training programs for youth.[3] Training programs began on a small scale during the early 1970s and expanded after the 1974–1975 recession. By 1976–77 over 117,700 16–18 year olds were covered by the major programs, which included (1) incentive training grants to provide training by employers or industrial training boards to meet future shortfalls at the technical or craft levels (42,900); (2) direct training and rehabilitation by the Training Services Administration (TSA) and Employment Service Agency (ESA) (15,000), both parts of the Manpower Services Commission (MSC); (3) work experience programs where trainees were placed in job situations (8,000); (4) special job creation administered by local authorities and community groups (21,000); and (5)subsidized jobs with private employers (30,300).

Initially these programs were adopted as temporary measures, but it has become apparent that the problems they address are more long term. In the spring of 1978 the Youth Opportunities Program (YOP) was launched incorporating several of the earlier programs, and by 1981 it included 360,000 places for 16 and 17 year olds, the largest number 242,000 being for Work Experience on Employer's Premises (WEEP). The earlier training programs of the TSA have also been expanded to provide 55,500 places for young people in a variety of employment induction, short training, and remedial courses. Projections are that during the 1982–83 year over 630,000 places will be provided under these various schemes.

Several smaller programs have also been introduced, including Unified Vocational Preparation (UVP), the Training for Skills Program (TSP), and the Young Workers Scheme (YWS). The UVP pays college fees and incentive grants to employers to provide extra training to young people who enter jobs that ordinarily have little or no further education requirements. The program is targeting 18,000 entrants for 1982–83, with substantial increases thereafter. The TSP subsidizes employers' wage and training costs, typically at a level of 50 percent. The YWS is a program whereby employers receive a weekly subsidy of 15 pounds for young workers who earn between 40 and 45 pounds a week and 7.50 pounds for those receiving less than 40 pounds per week.

In recent years continuing discussion has centered around a guarantee to all school leavers aged 16 and 17 that they receive either schooling, training, or a job. The MSC's *Youth Task Group Report* outlines a scheme whereby opportunities for all 16 year olds and those 17 year olds who have become unemployed within the first year of leaving school will be guaranteed training places by September 1983. Sponsors for the training positions will include private employers, local authorities, local education authorities, voluntary organizations, and industrial training boards.

Sweden

Although Sweden is by far the smallest country included in this study and a country with a relatively small youth unemployment problem (as of February 1981 unemployment in the 16–19-year-old group was only

8.7 percent, rising from 5.8 percent in 1980), its concern with youth unemployment has been the most pervasive of any country.[4] Sweden has curtailed its extensive apprenticeship system and progressively increased the proportion of young people attending upper secondary school. Today approximately 80 percent of its young people complete comprehensive high school, with one-half pursuing specializations. Despite the removal of these youngsters from the job market, the remaining youth have experienced increasing difficulties in obtaining jobs. Special programs were introduced, including work relief at market wages. By 1979–80, Sweden was employing 50,000 young persons on public projects. An additional 20,000 participated in special education and training measures. But in the summer of 1980 the government adopted a measure making 16 and 17 year olds the responsibility of the school system and authorized an expansion of school and college facilities.

In addition, vocational introduction to work and work preparation courses were introduced outside the schools. Vocational introduction was similar to the work experience programs in the United Kingdom, lasting up to 40 weeks. Young persons received the same allowance they would if they were attending school. In this way students were encouraged to remain in school rather than leave for higher-paying jobs. Union opposition to the low remuneration led to the development of new programs acceptable to both employees and trade unions.

On December 23, 1981, a new special agreement was reached between the Swedish Employers' Confederation (SAF) and the Swedish trade unions to provide special opportunities for 16 and 17 year olds whenever mutually agreeable to the employers and the unions. These jobs were to be open to young people who would otherwise not obtain places at high school or ordinary jobs for a specified period not to exceed six months, at a compensation of 85 Swedish kroner per day subsidized by the government.

France

Although the apprenticeship tradition began in France during the Middle Ages and has survived, it has not undergone the transformations that occurred in Germany and the United Kingdom.[5] Legislation to create technical and vocational education had been passed in 1919, and a system of apprenticeship tax was passed in 1925. But not until 1971 was a comprehensive training system established, by the passage of four major laws governing apprenticeship, technical education, further vocational training, and continuing education. When youth unemployment began climbing in the mid–1970s, efforts were made to adapt this training system to the needs of youth. From March 1968 to March 1974, unemployment among those less than 25 rose gradually from 3.2 percent to 4.9 percent. By March 1975 it had jumped to 7.9 percent.

Law No. 71–575 of July 16, 1971, on the Organization of Continuing Vocational Training Within the Framework of Education Permanente sets forth the right of employees to receive training and the obligation of employers to finance it. It is based upon the National Inter-Trade Agreement of 1970, which was subscribed to by both the employer and the trade union associations. The employer's obligation is fixed according to a percentage of the payroll and can be satisfied by providing training within the enterprise, signing an agreement with a training institution, contributing to the financing of the Training Insurance Fund, paying subsidies to designated vocational training institutions, or remitting money directly to the Public Treasury. The government has also accepted an obligation to provide additional funding.

While this basic system of training was conceived in times of business expansion, it provided the framework for changes necessitated by the rising unemployment of the mid–1970s. In late January 1975, the government launched the first program aimed at the growing number of unemployed young persons, Operation 50,000 Young Persons. By May 31, 16,400 young people were receiving training. The employment-training contract was introduced on an experimental basis as a cyclical measure on June 4, 1975. An important breakthrough in governmental policy occurred through Law No. 76–656 of July 16, 1976. It allowed the training fund financed by employer contributions to be used for funding programs for those seeking employment. Widespread opposition from the trade unions and training organizations developed. Nonetheless, this important principle was incorporated in the measures adopted in July of 1977, financed in part from the state budget and in part from a mandatory levy of .2 percent of total wages for firms participating in the financing of continuing vocational training and an exceptional contribution of .1 percent of the total wages for 1976. A similar approach was followed for similar measures adopted for 1978–79 and 1979–80.

This series of three sets of measures came to be referred to as Les Pactes Nationaux pour l'Emploi and included a variety of measures involving exemptions from paying employee social insurance, direct payments to companies, subsidies for apprenticeships, and vocational training. One of the most innovative efforts was a measure to provide practical training for persons between 16 and 25 in firms. The firms provide the training while the government pays monthly allowances to the beneficiaries. Employment-training contracts, upgrading courses organized by the National Employment Agency, and retraining courses and apprenticeship aid were also continued.

Currently the Socialist government is developing a new program with its own orientation. The program attempts a comprehensive approach to youth. In principle it is similar to the efforts of the United Kingdom and Sweden to provide a guarantee to all 16–18 year olds of either education or a professional credential. It also speaks of providing 100,000 high-quality training places for this group.

Japan

Japan has maintained low youth unemployment even without the aid of an apprenticeship system like Germany's.[6] The attention given to youth unemployment in the Western European countries and the United States is reserved in Japan for middle-aged workers. This difference is reflected in the attitudes of large corporations toward hiring young people. Dating back to the beginning of the twentieth century, Japan developed a strong tradition of training new workers. This tradition has been reinforced by the system of compensation based on seniority. Some Japanese companies still operate their own secondary school, reminiscent of the era when they actively recruited youngsters at 14 years of age.

Despite the distinctive attitude of Japanese companies in wanting to hire young persons, the dramatic rise in schooling of the Japanese population is affecting corporate hiring practices. Most Japanese now complete secondary school, with rising numbers completing university. Companies will adapt their hiring practices, but the disposition to hire the young still seems strong.

As a result of the low rates of youth unemployment in Japan, government has not adopted specific measures. How long the combination of low general unemployment and built-in preference for the young will maintain the situation is uncertain. For the immediate future, the demand for young workers presents a sharp contrast to the situation in other countries.

Summary

The involvements of the British, French, and Swedish governments, then, in the problems of youth unemployment have been continuous since the mid–1970s. A consensus seems to be emerging about the need to focus on 16 and 17 year olds and to provide some sort of guarantee covering education, training, and jobs. German involvement has been mostly directed at strengthening the apprenticeship program, although certain programs for special groups have been enacted. U.S. involvement, begun in the 1960s, focused mostly on training for the disadvantaged and temporary public sector jobs. It has diminished since the 1980 election of the Reagan administration. Japan has not taken any government action since the labor market for youth has remained strong.

THE ROLE OF EMPLOYER FEDERATIONS AND TRADE UNIONS

Employer and union groups have taken varying positions and roles with respect to these measures. They are ordinarily represented on the national level by confederations. In every country under study here, a central confederation of employers can be identified, representing if not all employers then at least a substantial portion of them and speaking for employers' interests. Among the trade unions there may be more than one confederation. The range of involvement of these confederations includes taking public stands, lobbying for positions, pressing their views through party channels, participating in policy making through ad hoc and regularly established groups, and assuming a role in the implementation of specific programs.

The position that these groups assume on any particular issue depends upon a number of factors, including local history, the composition of the organizations, their relationship to the governing party, and specific political circumstances. While these organizations may accept a general social obligation to help solve the youth unemployment problem, they are constrained by the views of their members.

In the case of the employer confederations, many of the constituent organizations are eager neither to accept the financial burden for training youth in their companies nor to sanction the government expenditures required for public support of such programs. If the confederation does agree on supporting measures to combat youth unemployment, should it favor direct action by employers or by the government? The burdens falling on companies to administer programs themselves and to accept responsibility for finding jobs or training places may be great and lead to adverse public reaction if they are not successful. To the extent that they urge government to act, they avoid taking action themselves. So the problem takes less of their own time, effort, and resources. But the danger to the employer associations is that government may adopt a policy that in the end either directly affects them by imposing taxes and regulations or involves expenditures increasing their overall tax burden. This may account for the increasingly activist stance of some associations. While the trade unions are uniform in proposing to solve youth unemployment through general economic policies to stimulate the economy and create jobs, the adoption of specific youth unemployment measures poses a dilemma for them, too. To the extent that measures employ young people, the unions run the risk of reducing the number of jobs open to their own membership. If there are a limited number of jobs, young people are competing with older workers. In a time of high general unemployment, it is difficult for unions to support measures that in effect provide preferential treatment for youth. In addition, if young workers are added to the work force at less than regular wages, they may adversely affect the ability of unions to secure higher wages for their members.

United States

When the Great Society resulted in an expansion of programs under the Manpower Development and Training Act (MDTA), labor and business were generally supportive. The original purpose of MDTA was to provide training for workers displaced by automation, a goal to which both the American Federation of Labor and Congress of Industrial Organizations (AFL-CIO) and the U.S. Chamber of Commerce (USCC) could subscribe. Both organizations were considerably cooler toward the Economic Opportunity Act (EOA), although it was supported by the AFL-CIO as part of the War on Poverty. Business responded positively to President Johnson's specific call for cooperation and developed some private sector training programs. It is noteworthy that it was necessary to create a special organization, the National Alliance for Business (NAB), since the U.S. Chamber of Commerce was not deemed appropriate for such a task. Some labor unions became positively involved by sponsoring training programs themselves. As the poverty program spread, and with the recession of the late 1960s, problems began to develop.

Businesses, affected by a loss of jobs, were not eager to hire disadvantaged youth. While some organizations like the NAB remained in operation and continued to generate some placements, private sector involvement decreased. The major supporters of MDTA came from the local community organizations, who received contracts to provide training programs. The attitude of the regular school system was mixed. Even though they received contracts under the legislation, they viewed the Department of Labor involvement in this area competitively.

When the Comprehensive Employment and Training Act of 1973 (CETA) was enacted, business organizations remained largely passive. The AFL-CIO had strongly supported the Emergency Employment Act of 1971 and now sought to increase that program dramatically. They believe that public sector job creation is justified when the private sector is unable to generate sufficient jobs. At their suggestion, safeguards were adopted to ensure that regular workers were not displaced, wages were not below legal minimum or prevailing rates, employees received the same benefits as other workers, and labor organizations commented on local applications. However, they distinguish public sector job creation programs from training programs for the disadvantaged, which they also favor. They are wary, however, of training programs that do not lead to jobs.

Under MDTA, policy makers in the legislative and executive branches of the federal government involved representatives of organized labor in the implementation process. For several years before CETA, the AFL-CIO and several major national unions provided services under contract to promote training and employment objectives. With the decentralization under CETA, the emphasis shifted to work at the local level. Both national contract efforts and local contract efforts developed to facilitate training and placement of CETA participants. The Human Resources Development Institute (HRDI) has operated similarly to its counterpart, the NAB, in promoting participation of labor unions in CETA. Most recently its efforts have devoted to support of the PICs. Labor participation was mandated on the planning council for the prime sponsor, and annual plans were to be submitted for review to labor organizations in the local areas representing employees engaged in work similar to that proposed to be funded. The main concerns of labor union representatives involved: the use of PSE workers for work otherwise done by regular employees, training disadvantaged workers in occupations for which a surplus of labor already existed, proposed PSE jobs that were below the prevailing rate for similar work performed by regular employees, and training programs that would not provide adequate skills or lead to unsubsidized employment. These concerns increased after the 1978 amendments reduced the wage rates.

In 1978, when the private industry councils (PICs) were introduced, the AFL-CIO again stated its fears that wages and labor conditions might be adversely affected. Labor unions were accorded a special role in the PICs, although they were dominated by business representatives. While two-thirds of the members were from business, labor representation constituted about 8 percent—in over 50 percent of the cases the statutory minimum of one member. On the whole these representatives see an important role for labor on these councils and an important task in encouraging private sector participation in CETA.

In the end, while the U.S. Chamber of Commerce and the AFL-CIO have been cognizant of the problem of youth unemployment, they have not taken the initiative to make suggestions or strongly supported the programs that were developed. Business groups by and large have viewed the programs skeptically, complaining about the poor quality of the participants and decrying their substantial cost. Labor unions too have been critical of the failure of the programs and their potential for displacing jobs. The unions, like the employers, emphasize the importance of a sound economy, although they suggest different routes. Neither group has spoken out against the demise of CETA. On the whole they have conducted themselves like classic interest groups: commenting on proposed policy, criticizing where they felt their interests were hurt, and not seeking to assume a positive role in implementation.

Federal Republic of Germany

The traditional interest group orientation of the American confederations is in stark contrast to that of the German confederations. Both employer and trade union groups participate in tripartite governance (along with the *Lander*) of the Federal Vocational Training Institute and control the apprenticeship programs at the local level. The 69 Chambers of Commerce and Industry operating throughout the country examine all new apprentices and monitor the operation of apprenticeships in their area. The Association of German Chambers of Industry and Commerce (DIHT) serves as the employers' federation and has quasi-official status, sanctioned by statute. The German trade unions participate actively in the apprenticeship program. As parties to the collective bargaining agreements that regulate the conditions of apprenticeship, they monitor the operation of apprenticeships and register complaints when they feel they are not being administered in the interest of the participants.

The Training Places Promotion Act of 1976, which threatened companies with a tax to support additional training places if they were not forthcoming, was opposed by the companies, which saw it as unnecessary interference. It functioned as a threat to the employers that was never imposed. With the recent law eliminating the threat to employers to impose a tax for training places, the system has returned to its former equilibrium. But the passage of the legislation and its aftermath demonstrated the central role of the employers in policy matters. Both employers and trade unions accept their roles in the system and their obligations. They also jointly resist federal government intervention beyond its current ministerial role.

United Kingdom

The Trades Union Congress (TUC) and the Confederation of British Industries (CBI) represent the trade unions and employers, respectively, in all policy matters, including those relating to youth unemployment. While their members compete vociferously in collective bargaining, they have also developed cooperative relationships in some training endeavors. The tradition of employer and trade union involvement in the training area has included joint involvement in apprenticeships through the collective bargaining process; joint involvement in the industrial training boards, which have included training programs for all workers; and cooperation with the Manpower Services Commission, which administers special training programs.

One of the issues on which the confederations have disagreed is the continuation of apprenticeships. TUC has sought to reduce the period of apprenticeship and raise remuneration. Employers have sought to increase their flexibility while maintaining the length of the training period. As a result an impasse has developed in which both employers and trade unions have deemphasized the apprenticeship program. When British youth unemployment rose during the 1970s, there was little support for expanding the apprenticeship system among either business or labor groups. Instead, a variety of special programs was instituted.

By 1981 under the Youth Opportunities Program (YOP) work experience had emerged as the dominant form of youth program. British employers responded remarkably well in placing young persons in positions for which they received a small government stipend while gaining work experience. The trade unions monitored these schemes closely to ensure they did not result in the loss of jobs.

As youth unemployment increased during 1981, the Manpower Services Commission (MSC) evolved a new, expanded version of the Work Experience on Employer's Premises (WEEP) program to focus on 16 and 17 year olds, providing longer-term training opportunities on a regular basis. It then proposed that a task force including business and labor representatives come up with concrete suggestions. These groups agreed upon a common proposal that was accepted by the government. It calls for a massive training program to be supported by government funds providing stipends and subsidizing in-company training. Local training boards having representatives from business and industry as well as local authorities will be responsible for approving programs. In effect, this new approach has involved the CBI and TUC in the policy-making process. It also promises to enhance their role in the implementation phase.

Sweden

The Swedish Employers' Confederation (SAF) and the Confederation of Swedish Trade Unions (LO) are deeply concerned about youth unemployment. Until recently it was the government, however, that developed and implemented policy. The first main policy of the Swedish government directed at youth unemployment was a program of public works jobs. While the trade unions favored this approach, the employers often criticized the "make-work" nature. This program was curtailed during the summer of 1980, when 16 and 17 year olds were made the responsibility of the schools and education and training programs were increased. As jobs have become scarcer, both employers and unions have supported increased educational and training opportunities.

More recently, vocational introduction programs have been mounted that provided up to 40 weeks of experience in companies for unemployed youth, who received stipends equal to those attending school. Following the earlier emphasis on education and training, it was argued that students should not be given an incentive to leave school. The unions objected to this program and favored the earlier program of work relief. In fact, the question of rate of pay has been at the center of the disagreement between the employers, favoring programs at lower rates, and the unions, favoring programs at higher rates.

The agreement of December 1981 to provide jobs for 16 and 17 year olds brought together the employees and the trade unions to agree upon a common approach. Active negotiations between the LO and SAF led to an agreement to achieve mutual objectives. The major controversy over wages was resolved by allowing a significantly higher stipend than students receive, but one considerably lower than the wage for full-time work. This case of assumption by employees and unions of policy making by delegation is similar to the British model emulating the German model. Currently negotiations are underway to provide a similar program for the 18–20-year-old age group.

France

Although employer groups and trade unions in France have developed a collaborative approach to making policy in the training area (highlighted by the National Inter-Trade Agreement of 1970), this approach has not yet been extended to the problem of youth unemployment. So far both groups have adopted a more traditional interest group stance. While the employers association, Conseil National du Patronat Français (CNPF), has generally supported Les Pactes Nationaux pour l'Emploi, the employee organizations have been critical. Following the adoption of the first measures in 1977, the unions reacted strongly. The Confédération Générale du Travail (CGT) opposed the pact and recommended in its stead a massive new employment program involving boosting public consumption, improving working conditions, repatriating jobs, reducing working hours, and cutting back on public services. The Confédération Générale des Cadres (CGC) felt that the measures had been designed with one eye to the election, making confrontation inevitable between the social partners.

Even more so than in other countries, both employers and trade unions support further education as a way of dealing with youth unemployment in France. The French reverence for education is great, and the espousal of more education is a common theme across the political spectrum. A new program developed by the Socialist government is currently being developed with trade union support. It appears to rely largely upon education and training. It does, however, recognize the importance of professional training and reflects the general European support for a youth guarantee. So far the active policy-making role assumed by the associations in the inception of the 1971 training institutions has not been adopted with respect to the youth employment issue.

Japan

Training of young people in Japan is handled by and large by the companies through their training programs. The unions that are organized on a company-by-company basis participate in the formulation of training policy. Unlike the German trade union involvement in apprenticeships, the Japanese trade unions do not become involved in training curricula or direction. Trade unionists and their leadership are thoroughly steeped in company policy and generally supportive.

In their approach to problems of unemployment among middle-aged workers, these groups have demonstrated their ability to cooperate with government officials. The strength of consensual politics seems even greater than in Germany.

CONFEDERATIONS OF EMPLOYERS AND TRADE UNIONS AS INTEREST GROUPS

We have now surveyed the development of policy responding to youth unemployment in six countries over a period of approximately ten years. In each of these countries an employers' confederation is identifiable that represents a significant proportion of the country's employers. The German Chambers of Industry and Commerce are unique in that they have a statutory basis and perform important responsibilities in approving and monitoring apprenticeship programs. The U.S. Chamber of Commerce is the weakest of the employer organizations; it is the least inclusive and has the most competition in the form of other business federations and ad hoc groups that are active politically at the national level. In all countries the trade unions belong to a small number of federations that are active at the national level, often only one or two. France, which has five major trade union confederations, is unusual.

All of the confederations of employers and trade unions are active politically: taking public stands, lobbying for their positions, and pressing their views through party channels. In Germany, the United Kingdom, and Sweden, the confederations of employers and trade unions have actively participated in policy making regarding youth unemployment. In France they participated in establishing a training system in 1971 but have so far not become involved in making policy specifically relating to youth unemployment. In Germany the confederations of employers and trade unions accept formal responsibilities in the implementation of the apprenticeship program.

The movement of these confederations beyond the role of traditional interest groups has important implications for interest group theories as well as for more general theories of government. While posing a dilemma for those concerned with democratic control, it also suggests an approach to making government less interventionist and more effective. It reflects a more general acceptance of the power of big business and organized labor as "social partners" in the governance process. They are viewed as legitimate groups within the society that accept certain social obligations. The enlarged role they have assumed in policy affecting youth unemployment has at times amounted to delegation of policy-making responsibility to nongovernmental agencies, albeit under the watchful eye of the government.

While some democratic theorists may view this as a perversion of democratic ideals, the German example should give pause to such an interpretation. The system in Germany has evolved with minimal governmental regulation and maximum protection of the interests of the young, while promoting the interests of the corporations, trade unions, and society in general. It has reduced the government role to one of occasional intervenor. It has taken the government out of the business of tax collector and achieved a degree of social compliance that is extraordinary. Transferring this approach to other countries is not easy. The free rider problem posed by the companies that refuse to mount training programs, preferring to benefit from the results of other programs, poses a dilemma for most countries. In fact, France and the United Kingdom have both used training levies, allowing companies that develop their own training to deduct their costs from their total subscription.

But the broader principle seems to be unquestionably commendable. When a social problem demands solution, government decision makers are not necessarily the best qualified to formulate appropriate social policy. Reversing the roles of interest groups by accepting them as policy makers can be most effective if they are broad-based and legitimate. Employer and trade union confederations, particularly if they are inclusive, have these qualities. Involving these groups in the formulation of policy can pave the way for their involvement in policy implementation. This approach redefines government involvement to one of overseer and intervenor *in extremus*.

This view of active involvement of interest groups within the processes of policy formation and implementation diverges from the traditionally sharp distinction between the decision makers who make policy and the interest groups that attempt to influence the decision makers. Thus, the confederations of employers and trade unions are ordinarily viewed as suppliants, cajoling, threatening, or even bribing (both legally and illegally) the policy makers. Here they themselves become the policy makers.

Bachrach and Baratz in another context have already called attention to this breakdown of the dichotomy between decision-making government officials and private individuals.[7] They emphasize the importance of nongovernment officials in policy development. The case of youth employment policy provides evidence for a breakdown in this dichotomy in the subsequent stages of policy formation and implementation. In a reversal of roles, government officials influenced the agenda pursued by private decision makers. A broader conception of the public policy process is needed to encompass the interaction of social institutions and groups with government decision makers, who perform an important, but not exclusive role.[8] The unit of analysis shifts from regulations and laws to actual effective social policies. The relative impact of government on those social policies then becomes the focus for our attention. The dichotomy between policy makers and interest groups gives way to a broader investigation of social actors and their respective roles.

In all of the countries studied, confederations of employers and labor unions have been involved in the policy process. Their role is obviously much more critical than in many other areas. For the success of many initiatives will depend upon their active involvement and cooperation. Short of the German government's attempt to intimidate private firms by threatening them with a tax if they did not provide sufficient training places, little direct confrontation has ensued. More typically, a program has been enacted to entice private firms to hire young people, usually with minimal effect.

The experience in the area of youth unemployment policy demonstrates that interest groups sometimes act out of character and that activity may be extremely productive. Of course, the need for vigilance on the part of government is great. But the evidence indicates that employer and trade union confederations can assume a positive role in the promotion of the common good while protecting the interests of their member groups.

The employer and trade union confederations have accepted increasing responsibility for the expansion of training places for 16, 17, and 18 year olds. While some governmental intervention is necessary, the major responsibility for implementation of such a policy should rest with these organizations and their members. The limitations of government power to determine and implement unilaterally effective policy have been repeatedly demonstrated in the area of youth employment policy. The emphasis must now be placed on involving employer and union confederations directly.

NOTES

1. *See*, generally, David Bresnick, "CETA's Challenge to the Evaluation of Vocational Education," in *The Handbook of Vocational Education Evaluation*, ed. Carol Tittle and Theodore Abramson (Beverly Hills, Calif.: Sage, 1979); Joseph Ball, "CETA Planning and Implementation: Pouring New Federalism Into Old Bottles?" (Paper presented at the annual conference of the American Society for Public Administration, 1975); and Andrew Hahn, "Taking Stock of YEDPA," *Youth and Society* 2, no. 2 (December 1979): 237–261.

2. *See*, generally Bundesandstalt fur Arbeit, *Employment Policy in Germany: Challenges and Concepts for the 1980s* (Nurnberg, Germany: Bundesandstalt fur Arbeit, 1978); CEDEFOP, *Legislative and Regulatory Structure of Vocational Training Systems* (Berlin: CEDEFOP, 1980). This material is also based upon field interviews and other materials.

3. *See*, generally, Manpower Services Commission (MSC), *Young People and Work* (London: MSC, May 1977); MSC, *A New Training Initiative* (London: MSC, May 1981); MSC, *Youth Task Group Report* (London: MSC, April 1982). This material is also based upon field interviews and other materials.

4. *See*, generally, Birgitta Magnusson, *What Is Being Done in Sweden for Unemployed 16 and 17 Year Olds* (Stockholm: Swedish Institute, 1981); Nordic Council of Ministers, *Youth Guarantee: Theory or Reality* (Stockholm: Secretariat of the Nordic Council of Ministers, June 1981). This section is also based upon field interviews and other materials.

5. *See*, generally, CEDEFOP, *Descriptions of the Vocational Training Systems, France* (Berlin: CEDEFOP, n.d.); France, Ministère du Travail et de la Participation, *Travail et emploi* (Paris: October 1981); Bernard Schwartz, *L'Insertion professionelle et sociale des jeunes* (Paris: La Documentation Française, September 1981).

6. *See*, generally, Haruo Shimada, *The Japanese Employment System* (Tokyo: Japan Institute of Labour, 1980). This material is also based upon field interviews and other materials.

7. Peter Bachrach and Morton S. Baratz, *Power and Poverty* (New York: Oxford University Press, 1970).

8. This point is developed further and its relationship to the growing debate about corporatism is discussed in David Bresnick, "The Youth Employment Policy Dance: Some Evidence for the Efficacy of Corporatism" (Paper delivered at the American Political Science Association meeting, Denver, 1982).

CHAPTER 9

The YOUTHJOBS Strategy

THE UNMET NEED

If government action in the past has been grandiose and ineffective, it has nonetheless responded to a real need. The youth labor market reflects a multitude of corporate, governmental, and individual decisions. Historical happenstance has much to say, as do demographic trends and the general state of the economy. Youth unemployment only becomes a problem when the supply of labor in the economy as a whole exceeds the demand. It is then shaped by a variety of other problems that confront the country and its employers.

Young workers as a group are experiencing increasing difficulty in the job market, and the disadvantaged are hit hardest. This has resulted in part from the general increase in the supply of labor and in part from the disappearance of low-skilled manufacturing and other jobs for which youth were sought because of their greater physical stamina. In addition, the wage differential for youth has been eroded in some countries by minimum wage legislation and union contracts. Given the need for initial investment in skill training and work socialization, companies are less inclined to hire youth when they can hire more mature or experienced workers at comparable wages. Within the United States, corporations with the most desirable career positions are limiting their hiring to those in their mid-twenties.

Japan seems to be the country with the strongest youth labor market. In the post–World War II period it was helped by the needs of an expanding economy. Corporations were hard pressed to obtain workers and looked toward those leaving school as a logical and abundant source. Demand for labor has remained high, while Japanese youth are attending secondary school and university in great numbers. Unemployment problems that do exist in Japan center around middle-aged and older workers.

Germany has also evolved an effective mechanism for placing youth in jobs and provides more systematic training than the Japanese. The apprenticeship system provides a ready mechanism for moving school leavers into the world of work. In 1976, when that system was threatened by a large number of school leavers and a decrease in training positions, the Training Places Promotion Act was adopted, resulting in an increase in training places. This government action and the corporate response provides a successful example of changing social policy through a process of mutual accommodation.

Historical circumstance has had a different impact on the United States. The overall unemployment rate has remained fairly high since the middle 1960s, and companies have been faced with a surplus of available labor. They have tended to hire experienced, mature workers, making it increasingly difficult for school leavers to obtain career positions. Corporate leadership tends to view youth as irresponsible, unreliable, militant, and mobile—all characteristics that make them less preferred as employees. Furthermore, corporate leadership has not generally viewed the problem of youth unemployment as an important social issue.

While the Congress has been extremely active in passing employment and training legislation, particularly focusing on the disadvantaged, the effectiveness of specific programs in increasing the lifetime earnings of participants has not been dramatic. Of course, the huge scale of training programs in certain periods did remove large numbers of youth from the labor market. An OECD report has even credited these programs with contributing to a reduction in youth unemployment.

Since the corporate sector was not involved in the policy-making process and is intent upon minimizing government regulation, it has not been eager to risk government intervention by participating in government-subsidized training programs. In fact, government regulatory activity in the related areas of employment of minorities and women, which has engendered the enmity and attention of corporate leaders, has even been cited as an excuse for not getting involved in youth employment issues.

Congressional activity to provide tax incentives for hiring disadvantaged employees or providing additional training has not received widespread support. While such benefits have been claimed by a limited number of companies, most have not sought them. Part of the reason has been their short and uncertain duration. In addition, they are offered in isolation rather than as part of a well-conceived youth employment policy.

While the Employment and Training Administration developed a sizable staff to administer first the Manpower Development and Training Act (MDTA) and later the Comprehensive Employment and Training Act (CETA), it never became an active arm of the government to work with private industry in developing effective employment policies. Its constituency became the local prime sponsors and the community agencies responsible for training programs rather than the companies whose ultimate hiring power was critical.

If the history of youth unemployment policy in this country has been dismal in the post–World War II era, why not admit its impossibility and move on to the next issue? The simple answer is that the depth of the personal and societal problems posed by youth unemployment are difficult to ignore. Some commentators belittle youth unemployment and explain the rates now approaching 50 percent in some cities by citing the large numbers of students engaged in part-time work and the relatively small group of long-term unemployed. Yet a substantial group of our young people who for one reason or another do not attend college are left in limbo. Others attend college simply because they cannot obtain jobs. From the point of view of individual firms competing in the free market, this fact may not be of immediate consequence. But from the point of view of a society that must rest its future with its youth, the long-term implications are unacceptable. They may also affect the longer-range competitiveness of American firms in the international market by failing to develop the potential of these youngsters to bolster the work force.

Millions of youth between the ages of 16 and 24 must each year wait until they come of age to compete successfully in the job market and then are at a disadvantage compared with those who have continued in school. And of course, the youth who are affected most by this state of affairs are those from the poorest economic backgrounds. Furthermore, there is increasing evidence that even when recovery comes, the youth job market will not improve to any significant degree.

The current economic recession and its effects on the youth labor market are threatening to discourage a generation of Americans and distort corporate hiring practices. The continuing success of German and Japanese firms in their effective use of young workers should provide an object lesson. It is not accidental that they have the strongest economies among the industrial nations. The effective use of human resources are at the heart of effective business operations. Even in times of depressed economic conditions, effective planning anticipates the future, including the development of a skilled work force.

School leavers find themselves in an uncomfortable dilemma. They can find temporary work at low wages, often characterized by periods of unemployment, or they can return to school and accept part-time work at low wages. Many would-be school leavers are thus driven back to school. For those who are not prepared to return to school, however, it means waiting five or more years until a career position may be obtained, and then often they are in competition with a university graduate who, by virtue of a degree, if not actual training, will be in a superior competitive position. This is a high price to pay, especially for those who "drop out" entirely. For society it means the loss of valuable young people who could probably contribute considerably to corporate productivity and may now be discouraged and become acclimated to a life of unemployment or underemployment.

Some companies are beginning to realize that they may be the greatest losers of all. With a minimum investment, these school leavers can become valuable employees with job-specific skills and organizational loyalty to provide returns to the company over a long working career. One suspects that American companies lulled into a false sense of security by the surplus labor on the job market and confronted by a mobile labor market where training investment looks risky are missing an important opportunity to develop a most valuable human resource. If this is so, the ultimate losers are American business and the American economy. Meanwhile, we are losing half our youth, who are being taught that they are expendable, a lesson they will undoubtedly learn well. Thus school leavers—those who most seek adulthood and independence through work—are relegated to a life of uncertainty and dependence. What a tragic irony for America.

The problem faced by youth and by older persons reentering the job market is not a lack of skills but their relative position in a lengthening queue of the unemployed. The problem of youth employment, as the enactment of the Youth Employment Demonstration Projects Act (YEDPA) suggested, needs to be addressed separately from that of welfare mothers or displaced workers.

The shortcomings of our mechanisms for helping youth make the transition to the world of work have become more apparent as our general unemployment has persisted. Our vocational education system leaves much to be desired. Our training programs for school leavers have not been successful. Efforts to establish private sector on-the-job training (OJT) programs have fallen short of their goals. Many secondary school leavers, particularly those from minority backgrounds, are having increasing difficulties.

Nonetheless, there are some reasons for optimism. We have been willing to try a variety of programs, some of which have been successful. Youth graduating university and community college have by and large good success in finding employment. Many of our secondary school graduates do, after a period of job instability, find good career positions.

Many of those youth who have difficulty in finding career employment find part-time and temporary jobs that lead to career positions.

Part-time work in the United States is extensive. It is most concentrated at the university level but also penetrates the secondary schools. In fact, the statistics probably understate this phenomenon, since the low pay that students receive is often paid "off the books" to avoid the costs of social security and withholding taxes, an implicit if illegal subsidy program for youth.

This system has also facilitated the continuation in school of large numbers of students who might otherwise have been forced to leave school. It also provides an informal but effective means for easing the transition of youth to the world of work. The number of individuals who continue on after graduation in positions that had begun as part-time jobs increasingly accounts for the bulk of employment.

Capitalizing on the growth of part-time work opportunities, schools have taken the initiative in combining vocational education with OJT placements in private companies. In fact, the best programs that have developed in the United States at the local level have been surprisingly good. Secondary schools throughout the country have taken to encouraging part-time jobs either informally or through cooperative education programs administered as part of the curriculum.

Yet part-time jobs also pose real dilemmas. While they may provide valuable socialization to the world of work, they are usually in the secondary labor market. They require a minimum of skills, thus providing little opportunity for training and individual development. Workers are considered expendable and are easily replaced, so that the jobs tend to be temporary. Students may develop low job expectations, accepting poor working conditions, job instability, and low remuneration.

The widespread use of such jobs within the secondary labor market may in fact discourage companies from creating more responsible positions at higher pay that might lead to career prospects in the firm. The prospects of short-term profits through low labor costs may be too appealing to resist. Yet the needs of school leavers for developing careers and attachments to organizations and adults may thus be ignored.

We do not suffer from a lack of ideas but rather from the institutionalization of these ideas and their coordination. The last attempt to provide that coordination, the Youth Office of the Employment and Training Administration in the U.S. Department of Labor has disappeared. A multifaceted approach is needed to help all school leavers. We need to improve secondary education, including vocational education, and to encourage students to complete their degrees. Part-time jobs can be a potent incentive. We need to expand public sector and community-based job creation programs. But most importantly we need to develop a large-scale OJT program for those both leaving and completing secondary school who do not go on to community college or university.

In summary, we need a program for providing YOUTHJOBS for our young people. It is no longer enough to say that you are guaranteed a place in high school and community college. We must say you are guaranteed a learning opportunity in the real world of work that has a reasonable chance of becoming a job. Youth cannot expect better treatment than adults, but they can expect a real chance to be trained in a work situation with an expectation of employment. They want it, and it is in our interests to give it to them.

Such a program needs to be especially designed for American requirements. The rigidities of the German apprenticeship system and the male orientation of the Japanese system should be rejected. But we need some system that can provide large numbers of YOUTHJOBS so that young people who leave school at 16, 17, and 18, and even older can continue their transition to adult life. We must welcome them into our large and small work organizations and acknowledge their central role in our future.

What is needed is a policy that combines government action with private response. What is needed on the part of the government and the business community and the labor unions is a realization that the costs of excluding American youth from career employment are too great and that changes must be made. What is needed is a viable policy that will obtain the sanction and compliance of the major actors.

TOWARD A PRIVATE SECTOR SOLUTION

In assessing the viability of such an approach, one of the persistent questions is whether the American government and American business community are sufficiently well integrated to achieve the coordination required. Germany and Japan, the two major countries that most effectively integrate youth into their work forces, have a much stronger tradition of government and business working together. The United Kingdom and France, too, have much closer working relationships between business and government. In fact, the American predicament is complicated by the competition in recent years between the government and the business community.

Yet, in spite of the difficulties of achieving business and government collaboration within the United States, examples do emerge indicating that it can be achieved, if the problems to be confronted are viewed as serious enough. The collaboration that resulted in the institution of vocational education throughout the country in the early part of the twentieth century is one example. President Lyndon Johnson's efforts to create OJT slots through the National Alliance of Business (NAB) are another. The efforts of business to rebuild the central cities during the late 1960s are another.

There does seem to be some evidence that the NAB is gaining a new momentum and that the private industry councils (PICs) established under CETA are achieving some gains. The New York City Partnership mobilized business during the summer of 1981 to obtain part-time jobs for minority youth and is currently working on programs for full-time slots.

The first aspect of a policy that might change youth employment practices would be a statement of general purpose that would be adhered to by government and private business to the effect that changes in the youth employment market are necessary. This might be accompanied by a statement of hiring goals for the entire country or by states and local areas. Of course, in order for the statement to be effective it must be accepted by the business community as viable and justifiable, and a system of incentives and penalties must be enacted to ensure that the policy becomes implemented. Private corporations are unlikely to change their labor market habits of many years' standing unless some direct encouragement and incentives exist. Among the options to be considered are officially authorized lower wages for youth; direct subsidies for training programs for youth, especially those leading to more generalized skill development; technical assistance to companies implementing new programs; and the use of tax incentives to encourage training programs and career positions for youth.

Congressional legislation reflecting this approach could initially follow the Employment Act of 1946 and the Full Employment and Balanced Growth Act of 1978 (Humphrey-Hawkins). Like those laws, broad policy objectives should be articulated. The need to reorient the youth labor market to focus on career employment for school leavers should be clearly stated. The current Republican administration would be in an ideal position to involve business in such a commitment since it is in line with its own views of the need for voluntary action by individuals and corporations. The problem, of course, is that current evidence indicates that corporate leadership is not willing to hire youth into career positions when more mature or more experienced individuals are available.

As the Full Employment Act of 1946 and the Full Employment and Balanced Growth Act of 1978 demonstrated, pious language is not enough. Government action is necessary—but action that involves business and labor as responsible social partners who assume a joint obligation for the implementation of the program. What government must do is create a framework of incentives so that individual companies find it in their interest to invest in our young people. The cost of investing in young people must be made sufficiently attractive so that it is clearly in the interest of reluctant firms without experience in youth training programs to get involved. It would seem that the simplest and most direct method for doing that would be to legitimize a youth differential for paying young people a reduced stipend during a specified training period. Closely related to this concept is that the program must be viewed as a training program to attract and develop the best available talent. While business leaders neither want nor expect intellectual giants, neither do they relish being viewed as rehabilitation centers for the rejected. Any attempt to limit such a program to the "disadvantaged" is neither wise nor politic and will almost certainly lead to program failure.

On the surface it would seem that the German example provides better guidance than the Japanese system. It is unlikely that the establishment of a steeply graduated seniority wage system is practicable in the United States. The designation of a training period of two or three years for trainees would on the other hand be manageable. Of course, a formula acceptable to unions would be required.

The second major problem of incentives focuses around the "free rider" problem. Given the mobility of the labor market in the United States, which means that individuals trained in one company can leave for another, companies have little incentive to invest in training young people. Partly this may require reorientation of company policy to value youth trainees. It is rather certain, however, that additional measures will be necessary. The approach that the United Kingdom and France have used is a training assessment determined by a percentage of payroll. This tax is then refunded or never collected from companies that can document their expenditures for internal training of new workers.

Having established an environment in which corporations receive positive incentives to institute training programs for young workers, a further consideration should be some contribution to the quality of the training programs and some provision for encouraging cooperation of smaller firms. A public corporation financed out of the proceeds of the training fund, out of unemployment insurance itself, or as part of federal aid to education could be established to ensure that standards of these training programs are high. Although the Japanese system does not have such an entity, the German Federal Vocational Training Institute provides a model for such an organization. It also would save a good deal of money by avoiding the costs of developing duplicate curricula. While the approach taken by the Germans is sometimes criticized for its detail, it has actually achieved a remarkable sense of acceptance from both industry and labor and actively involves them both, in addition to the *Lander* in curriculum development.

In formulating an American response to the needs of our young people, the lessons of the past should not be forgotten. We do not need more cumbersome programs leading to ineffectual intervention by government in a largely private sector youth labor market. We need wise and joint response by business and labor nudged by our government to assume their rightful roles as social partners.

There are traditions to draw upon and precedents to follow. The rewards of success will be a reorientation of a large part of our youth from a future of uncertainty and despair to one of direction and productivity. A new policy encouraging the development of YOUTHJOBS will help them and help us all. It will provide a strong basis for a renewed national effort to keep America competitive in meeting the serious international economic challenges of the remaining part of the twentieth century.

THE YOUTHJOBS PROGRAM

Moving from the general to the specific is risky in the public policy area, particularly in an area as volatile as employment policy. The specifics of any policy should be subject to a process of bargaining among the interested parties. The importance of involving employers and trade unions in this bargaining process has been emphasized already. The following guidelines are suggested to guide the process of formulating a viable policy of YOUTHJOBS.

1. The program must be developed on a national basis. While allowance must be made for regional and local variation, the broad outlines of the policy must be agreed to in a national forum and be supported by the major national employer and trade union associations. All businesses must accept a financial obligation to support their share of the program.

2. The main focus of the program is to create large numbers of trainee positions in the major employing institutions in our society for young people between ages 16 and 19. The purpose of these traineeship positions is to provide work experience in productive organizations. Trainees should receive a stipend of approximately 25–50 percent of the wages of a beginning worker. A strong training component should be introduced involving both OJT and classroom training. Every effort should be made to ensure that at least 50 percent of the trainees are kept in regular jobs after the traineeship ends.

3. The program should include public service jobs providing an equivalent stipend. This component should be careful to emphasize placement in jobs, education, or training programs leading to realistic work options. It should avoid expansion beyond its placement capabilities. At least a portion of this program should be residential, focusing on community service projects and targeted at disadvantaged youth with low records of educational achievement.

4. Efforts should be made to improve the vocational introduction in upper secondary school for those in general educational programs and particularly for those not planning to continue their education. Students should be encouraged to accept part-time work, especially within the context of a cooperative education program supervised by the school and related to the career aspirations of the student.

5. Explicitly designated vocational tracks at the secondary school level should be required to demonstrate success in placing young people into the field for which they are preparing them. Special efforts should be made to arrange OJT in association with vocational education at the secondary level, to provide real work experience, and to ease the transition to work.

6. Current vocational guidance services for young people need to be strengthened. Consideration should be given to creating a special youth section within state-administered employment offices, with responsibility for close supervision of all 16, 17, and 18 year olds.

This YOUTHJOBS program clearly raises some difficult questions about administration and finance.

Administration

The most difficult administrative problems arise with respect to the new OJT traineeships in employing organizations. Primary responsibility should rest with local employers. Trade unions should have a responsibility for monitoring the programs to ensure that they are of high quality and do not result in the loss of full-time employment.

There is a further need for a local body to monitor the traineeship programs. In the German system this function is performed by the Chambers of Commerce and Industry, and in the proposed system in the United Kingdom it will be performed by the local boards, containing representation from among employers, trade unions, and education and training officials. The private industry councils (PICs) would be the most logical group in the United States to perform this role.

In addition, it may be that some national capability, modeled on the Federal Vocational Training Institute in Germany, is needed to facilitate curriculum development and to provide technical assistance to the individual employers. An alternative would be to set up a technical assistance office in each state.

One approach to the administration of public service jobs would be to expand the existing Job Corps. But while this program is highly successful and should be retained, other alternatives might be advisable. As in the United Kingdom, greater emphasis might be given to the establishment of community-based groups to develop programs on an ongoing basis. Indeed some such groups of varying quality have functioned under MDTA and CETA. Also public service employment might include nonresidential programs, which could be organized by a unit of state or local government. Where community groups or state and local or even national governmental units organize programs, they should bear primary administrative responsibility. They might then be responsible to the same local authorities monitoring the OJT program, described above.

Secondary schools, which should also take a more active role in vocationally oriented education, already have a set administrative organization in each state, including a special structure for vocational education. The responsibility for vocational guidance of 16, 17, and 18 year olds needs some attention. At present, many schools have vocational guidance counselors who have responsibility in this area. Students also come into contact with public employment services either on their own or through referral from unemployment or welfare offices. A real need exists for a more active approach to the employment of youth and for their referral to the new YOUTHJOBS. It is proposed that a new section within the Employment Service be organized to focus on 16–19 year olds, perhaps to be located within secondary schools. They should provide general career guidance on an individual and group basis as well as provide information on available education, training, YOUTHJOBS, and other full-time and part-time employment positions.

Finance

The program described above need not involve substantial expense beyond that already existing. The most marked change from the past would be the traineeships in the private sector, which present the greatest challenge. In the financing of these programs it must be kept in mind that they are basically designed to improve the capabilities of the work force. In this sense they are a logical cost of doing business, and in principle each employer should absorb the cost of providing traineeships.

While this approach works reasonably well in Germany, it would probably not work in the United States. Traditions here do not favor company investment in traineeship programs. In fact, companies are turning away from youth and are seeking to avoid the costs of initial training by hiring more experienced workers. High labor mobility encourages employers to be "free riders." Probably the only hope of encouraging businesses to accept the responsibility for providing traineeships is to assess them, whether or not they provide these services, as is the current practice in both France and the United Kingdom. The simplest approach would be to add a small additional percentage to the social security payroll tax. Companies that conducted their own training programs would then receive a waiver of the tax.

In order to encourage new approaches to training and in particular arrangements with local school systems to provide classroom training along with the traineeship, incentive grants might be provided, tapping federal funds currently provided for vocational training. In fact, consideration might be given to subsidize all training efforts by business using these funds, as distinct from the stipends that the trainees should receive directly from the employer. Insofar as is possible, the funding of the employment service should continue at the current levels. It may be necessary, however, to provide additional federal financing to initiate this new program targeted for 16–19 year olds.

In outlining this program of YOUTHJOBS, I have been bound by a strong sense of the possible. It will offend some groups and will arouse the support of others. But in judging it for yourself I hope you will temper self-interest with the needs of our young people. I believe that it is we who are currently failing them and that we are bearing the social costs of this failure.

YOUTHJOBS are no panacea for ending the problems of youth unemployment. As I have argued, a strong economy is the best guarantee of adequate jobs. But my nagging fear is that fundamental changes have taken place in the youth labor market. Given the levels of economic recovery we have a right to expect, our young people are threatened with being relegated indefinitely to a secondary labor market, receiving neither job security nor skills training. YOUTHJOBS can help change all that and lead us to a more productive future.

Bibliography

Ahlkvist, Birgitta. *Initial In-Plant Vocational and Technical Training in Sweden.* Stockholm: Swedish Employers Confederation, 1978.

Anderson, Bernard, and Sawhill, Isabel. eds. *Youth Employment and Public Policy.* Englewood Cliffs, N.J.: Prentice-Hall, 1980.

Ashenfelter, Orley, and Rees, Albert. *Discrimination in Labor Markets.* Princeton: Princeton University Press, 1973.

Ashton, D. N. "The Transition from School to Work: Notes on the Development of Different Frames of Reference Among Young Male Workers." *Sociological Review* 21 (1973): 101–125.

Ashton, D. N. and Field, David. *Young Workers.* London: Hutchinson, 1976.

Ball, Colin, and Ball, Meg. *Fit for Work? Youth, School and Employment.* London: Writers and Readers, 1979.

Ball, Joseph. "CETA Planning and Implementation: Pouring New Federalism Into Old Battles?" Paper presented at the annual conference of the American Society for Public Administration, 1975.

———. "The Implementation of Federal Manpower Policy, 1961–1971." Ph.D. dissertation, Columbia University, 1972.

———. *The Participation of Private Businesses as Work Sponsors in the Youth Entitlement Demonstration.* New York: Manpower Demonstration Research Corporation, 1981.

Ball, Joseph, et al. *The Quality of Work in the Youth Entitlement Demonstration.* New York: Manpower Demonstration Research Corporation, April 1980.

Ballon, Robert J., ed. *The Japanese Employee.* Rutland, Vt.: Charles Tuttle, 1969.

Bauer, David. *Factors Moderating Unemployment Abroad.* Studies in Business Economics, no. 113. New York: National Industrial Conference Board, 1970.

Benner, Herman. *Demarcation of Occupational Groups/Occupational Fields With Regard to Vocational Training at Skilled Level in the European Community.* Berlin: CEDEFOP, 1981.

Berg, Ivar. *Education and Jobs: The Great Training Robbery.* New York: Columbia University Press, 1970.

Berryman, Sue. "Youth Unemployment and Career Education: Reasonable Expectations." *Public Policy* 26, no. 1 (1978): 29–69.

Bildung und Wissenschaft. *Vocational Training in the Federal Republic of Germany*. Bonn: Inter Nationes, 1981.

Bird, Caroline. *The Case Against College*. New York: McKay, 1975.

Bishop, J. *Employment in Construction and Distribution Industries: The Impact of the New Jobs Tax Credit*. Madison, Wisc.: Institute for Research on Poverty, 1980.

Bolino, August C. *Career Education*. New York: Praeger, 1973.

Borus, Michael. *Measuring the Impact of Employment-Related Social Programs*. Kalamazoo, Mich.: W. E. Upjohn Institute for Employment Research, 1979.

Bowers, Norman. "Youth Labor Force Activity: Alternative Surveys Compared." *Monthly Labor Review* 9 (1981): 3–17.

Brannen, P. *Entering the World of Work: Some Sociological Perspectives*. London: Department of Employment, 1975.

Branscomb, L. M. and Gilmore, P. C. "Education in Private Industry." *Daedelus* (Winter 1975): 223.

Bresnick, David. "CETA's Challenge to the Evaluation of Vocational Education." In *The Handbook of Vocational Education Evaluation*, edited by Carol Tittle and Theodore Abramson. Beverly Hills, Calif.: Sage, 1979.

———. "The Youth Employment Policy Dance: Some Evidence for the Efficacy of Corporatism." Paper delivered at the American Political Science Association meeting, Denver, 1982.

Bundesandstalt fur Arbeit. *Employment Policy in Germany: Challenges and Concepts for the 1980s*. Nurnberg, Germany: Bundesandstalt fur Arbeit, 1980.

Cahiers du Centre d'Etudes de l'Emploi. *L'Entree dans la vie active*. Paris: Presses Universitaires de France, 1976.

———. *Les Jeunes et l'emploi*. Paris: Presses Universitaires de France, 1975.

Carnegie Council on Policy Studies on Higher Education. *Giving Youth a Better Chance: Options for Education, Work and Services*. San Francisco: Jossey-Bass, 1979.

Carter, M. P. *Home, School and Work*. Oxford: Pergamon Press, 1962.

Casson, Mark. *Youth Unemployment*. London: Macmillan, 1979.

CEDEFOP. *Descriptions of the Vocational Training Systems*. Berlin: CEDEFOP, n.d.

———. *Legislative and Regulatory Structure of Vocational Training Systems*. Berlin: CEDEFOP, 1980.

Centre d'Etudes et de Recherches sur les Qualifications. *Les Emplois femmes par les jeunes de 17 ans*. Paris: La Documentation Française, 1972.

Clarke, H. F. and Sloan, H. S. *Classroom in the Factories*. New York: New York University Press, 1958.

Cohen, Eli, and Kapp, Louise. *Manpower Policies for Youth*. New York: Columbia University Press, 1966.

Coleman, James, et al. *Youth: Transition to Adulthood*. Washington, D.C.: Office of Science and Technology, Executive Office of the President, June 1973.

Commission of the European Communities. Directorate General for Research, Science and Education. *From Education to Working Life*. Brussels: Commission of the European Communities, 1980.

Committee for Economic Development. *Jobs for the Hard-to-Employ: New Directions for a Public-Private Partnership.* New York: Committee for Economic Development, January 1978.

Community Council of Greater New York. *Job Prospects for Urban Youth: Strategies for the 1980's.* New York: New York City Youth Employment Conference, February 1980.

Community Task Force. *Annual Report and Accents.* London: Community Task Force, 1980–1981.

Conant, James B. *Slums and Suburbs.* New York: McGraw-Hill, 1961.

Cook, Fred. "Opportunities and Requirements for Initial Employment of School Leavers with Emphasis on Office and Retail Jobs." Ph.D. dissertation, Wayne State University, 1966.

Davis, Russell. *Education and Employment.* Lexington, Mass: Lexington Books, 1975.

Diaz, William, et al. *The Youth Entitlement Demonstration: Second Interim Report on Program Implementation.* New York: Manpower Demonstration Research Corporation, 1980.

Doeringer, Peter, ed. *Workplace Perspective on Education and Training.* Boston: Martinus Nijhoff, 1981.

Doeringer, Peter, and Vermeulen, Bruce. *Jobs and Training in the 1980's.* Boston: Martinus Nijhoff, 1981.

Dohnanyi, Klaus von. *Education and Youth Employment in the Federal Republic of Germany.* Berkeley, Calif.: Carnegie Council on Policy Studies in Higher Education, 1978.

Dynamit Nobel. *Werkzreitshrift*, no. 5 (1981).

European Centre for the Development of Vocational Training. *Vocational Training.* Berlin: CEDEFOP, 1978.

Farine, Avigdor. *Les Liens entre la formation et l'emploi en France, en Allemagne, en Italie et en Espagne.* Montreal: Faculté des Sciences de L'Education, 1979.

Fearn, Robert. "Labor Force and School Participation of Teenagers." Ph.D. dissertation, University of Chicago, 1967.

Federal Employment Institute. *Employment Policy in Germany: Challenges and Concepts for the 1980s.* Nurnberg, Germany: Federal Employment Institute, 1978.

Feldstein, Martin. "The Economics of the New Unemployment." *Public Interest*, no. 33 (1973): 3–42.

———. "The Private and Social Costs of Unemployment." *American Economic Review* (May 1978): 155–164.

Fisher, Alan Aron. "The Problem of Teenage Unemployment." Ph.D. dissertation, University of California at Berkeley, 1968.

Fondation Europeénne de la Culture. *Between School and Work.* Amsterdam: Institute of Education, 1976.

France. Ministère du Travail. Agence Nationale Pour L'Emploi. *Mèsures pour L'Emploi et la formation des jeunes: Loi du 5 juillet 1977.* Paris: Dossier Technique, 1977.

France. Ministère du Travail et de la Participation. *Travail et emploi.* Paris: Service des Etudes et de la Statistique, October 1981.

Freeberg, Norman. "Criterion Measures for Youth-Work Training Programs: The Development of Relevant Performance Dimensions." *Journal of Applied Psychology* 61, no. 5 (1976): 537–545.

Freedman, Marcia. *Labor Markets: Segments and Shelters*. Montclair, N.J.: Allanheld, Osmun, 1976.

Freeman, R., and Wise, David H. "The Youth Employment Problem: Its Dimensions, Causes and Consequences." Paper presented at the NBER Conference on Youth Joblessness and Unemployment, Airlie House, Va., July 17–18, 1979.

Freeman, Richard B. *Why Is There a Youth Labor Market Problem?* Cambridge, Mass.: National Bureau of Economic Research, 1979.

Gilli, Angelo. *Modern Organization of Vocational Education*. University Park: Pennsylvania State University Press, 1976.

Ginzberg, Eli, ed. *Employing the Unemployed*. New York: Basic Books, 1980.

Glover, Robert. *Apprenticeship in the United States: Implications for Vocational Education Research*. Columbus, O.: National Center for Research in Vocational Education, 1980.

Gordon, David. *Theories of Poverty and Underemployment*. Lexington, Mass.: Heath, 1972.

Gordon, Margaret. *Youth Education and Employment Problems: An International Perspective*. Berkeley, Calif.: Carnegie Council on Policy Studies in Higher Education, 1979.

Grasso, John. *The Contributions of Vocational Education, Training and Work Experience to the Early Career Achievements of Young Men*. Columbus: Ohio State University Center for Human Resources Research, 1975.

———, and Shea, John R. *Vocational Education and Training: Impact on Youth*. Berkeley, Calif.: Carnegie Council on Policy Studies in Higher Education, 1979.

Gregoire, Roger. *Vocational Education*. Paris: OECD, 1967.

Grünewald, Bjorn. *Creative School Makes Transition Into Working Life Easier*. Stockholm: Swedish Employers' Confederation, February 1980.

Hahn, Andrew. "Early Themes from YEDPA: The Federal Youth Employment Initiative—Part 2." Mimeographed, 1980.

———. "Taking Stock of YEDPA: The Federal Youth Employment Initiatives." *Youth and Society* 2, no. 2 (December 1979): 237–261.

Hamermesh, Daniel. *Economic Aspects of Manpower Training Programs*. Lexington, Mass: Heath, 1971.

Interface. Educational Priorities Panel. *Help Wanted: The Management Study of Public Vocational Education in New York City*. New York: Interface, July 1980.

International Labour Office. *Youth Training and Employment Schemes in Developing Countries: A Suggested Cost-Benefit Analysis*. Geneva: ILO, 1972.

Ishikawa, Toshio. *Vocational Training*. Tokyo: Japan Institute of Labor, 1981.

Japan. Prime Minister's Office. *Japanese Statistical Yearbook 1981*. Tokyo: Statistics Bureau, 1981.

Johnston, Jerome, and Jerald G. Bachman. *Report on Longitudinal Study of National Sample of Males in the High School Class of 1969*. D.L. 81–26–72-05. Washington, D.C.: Department of Labor, Manpower Administration.

Jurman, E. A. "Teenage Unemployment Crisis or Challenge?" *Thrust,* no. 3 (1981): 69–96.

Kalchek, Edward. *The Youth Labor Market.* Washington, D.C.: National Manpower Policy Task Force, 1969.

Kantor, Harvey, and David Tyack. *Work, Youth and Schooling.* Stanford: Stanford University Press, 1982.

Kato, Hidetoshi. *Education and Youth Employment in Japan.* Berkeley, Calif.: Carnegie Council on Policy Studies in Higher Education, 1978.

Kaufman, Jacob, et al. *The Role of Secondary Schools in Preparing Youth for Employment.* University Park: Institute for Research on Human Resources, Pennsylvania State University, 1967.

Lazerson, Marvin, and Grubb, W. Norton, eds. *American Education and Vocationalism* New York: Teachers College, 1974.

Lecht, Leonard. *Involving Private Employers in Local CETA Programs.* New York: Conference Board, 1979.

Levine, S. V. *The Psychological and Social Effects of Youth Unemployment.* Toronto: Center for Urban and Community Studies, University of Toronto, 1980.

Levitan, Sar, and Alderman, Karen. "The Military as an Employer." *Monthly Labor Review* 100 (1977): 19–23.

Levitan, Sar, and Johnston, Benjamin. *The Job Corps: A Social Experiment That Works.* Baltimore: Johns Hopkins University Press, 1975.

Levitan, Sar, and Taggart, Robert. *Emergency Employment Act: The PEP Generation.* Salt Lake City: Olympus, 1974.

Levy, Frank. "A Detailed Analysis of Youth Unemployment Statistics." U.S. Department of Labor/ASPER, J–9–M–8–0128.

Lusterman, Seymour. *Education in Industry.* New York: Conference Board, 1977.

————, and Gorlin, Harriet. *Educating Students for Work: Some Business Roles.* New York: Conference Board, 1980.

Maclure, Stuart. *Education and Youth Employment in Great Britain.* Berkeley, Calif.: Carnegie Council on Policy Studies in Higher Education, 1979.

Magnusson, Birgitta. *What Is Being Done in Sweden for Unemployed 16 and 17 Year Olds.* Stockholm: Svenska Institute, 1981.

Mangum, G. L. *MDTA, Foundations of Federal Manpower Policy.* Baltimore: Johns Hopkins University Press, 1968.

————, and Walsh, J. *A Decade of Manpower Development and Training Programs.* Salt Lake City: Olympus, 1973.

Manpower Demonstration Research Corporation. Board of Directors. *Summary and Findings of the National Supported Work Demonstration.* Cambridge, Mass: Ballinger, 1980.

Manpower Institute. *Study of Corporate Youth Employment Policies and Practices.* Washington, D.C.: Manpower Institute, 1973.

Manpower Services Commission. *A Framework for the Future.* London: MSC, July 1981.

————. *A New Training Initiative.* London: MSC, May 1981.

————. *Young People and Work.* London: MSC, May 1977.

————. *Young People on Work.* London: MSC, December 1981.

————. *Youth Task Group Report.* London: MSC, April 1982.

Marshall, Ray. "The Economics of Racial Discrimination: A Survey." *Journal of Economic Literature* (September 1984): 849–871.

———. *Employment of Blacks in the South.* Austin: University of Texas Press, 1978.

Mathematica Policy Research. *Evaluation of the Economic Impact of the Job Corps Program: Second Follow-up Report.* Princeton, N.J.: Mathematica Policy Research, April 1980.

———. *Evaluation of the Economic Impact of the Job Corps Program: Third Follow-up Report.* Princeton, N.J.: Mathematica Policy Research, September 1982.

McGowan, Eleanor Farrar, and Cohen, Daniel K. "Career Education—Reforming School Through Work." *Public Interest* (1976): 22–47.

Melvyn, P. "Youth Unemployment in Industrialized Market Economy Countries." *International Labour Review* 116 (1977): 23–38.

———, and Freedman, D. H. "Youth Unemployment: A Worsening Situation." In *International Labour Office Employment: Outlook and Insights*, pp. 81–92. Geneva: International Labour Office, 1979.

Mirengoff, William, and Rindler, Lester. *CETA: Manpower Programs Under Local Control.* Washington, D.C.: National Academy of Sciences, 1978.

Mirengoff, William, et al. *CETA: Accomplishments, Problems, Solutions.* Washington, D.C.: Bureau of Social Science Research, 1981.

National Academy of Education. *Education for Employment: Knowledge for Action: Report of the Task Force on Education and Employment.* Washington, D.C.: National Academy of Education, March 1979.

National Advisory Council on Vocational Education. *Youth Unemployment: The Need for a Comprehensive Approach.* Washington, D.C.: National Advisory Council on Vocational Education, 1977.

National Commission for Manpower Policy. *A Collection of Policy Papers Prepared for Three Regional Conferences.* Washington, D.C.: Government Printing Office.

———. *From School to Work.* Washington, D.C.: Government Printing Office, 1976.

———. *Increasing Job Opportunities in the Private Sector: A Conference Report.* Special Report No. 29. Washington, D.C.: Government Printing Office, 1978.

National Council on Employment Policy. "The Impact of Employment and Training Programs." In *Evaluation Studies Review Annual*, edited by M. Guttentag. Vol. 2. Beverly Hills, Calif.: Sage, 1977.

National Urban League. *To Be Young, Jobless and Black.* New York: National Urban League, 1977.

Nolfi, George, et al. *Experiences of Recent High School Graduates.* Lexington, Mass.: Heath, 1978.

Nordic Council of Ministers. *Youth Guarantee: Theory or Reality.* Stockholm: Secretariat of the Nordic Council of Ministers, June 1981.

Okochi, K., Karsh, B., and Levine, S. B. *Workers and Employers in Japan.* Tokyo: University of Tokyo Press, 1973.

Organization for Economic Cooperation and Development. *Entry of Young People Into Working Life.* Paris: OECD, 1977.

———. *The Future of Vocational Education and Training.* Paris: OECD, 1983.

————. *Labor Force Statistics, 1968–1979*. Paris: OECD, 1981.

————. *Youth Employment: Special Annotated Bibliography*. Paris: OECD, 1980.

————. *Youth Unemployment: Report on Two Joint Meetings of Management and Trade Union Experts*. Paris: OECD, 1979.

————. *Youth Unemployment: The Causes and Consequences*. Paris: OECD, 1980.

Ornstein, Michael D. *Entry Into the American Labor Force*. Toronto: York University Press, 1976.

Osterman, Paul. *Getting Started: The Youth Labor Market*. Cambridge, Mass: MIT Press, 1980.

————. "Youth, Work and Unemployment." *Challenge* (May–June, 1978).

Panel of Consultants on Vocational Education (Benjamin Willis et al.). *Education for a Changing World of Work*. Washington, D.C.: Government Printing Office, 1963.

Pate, Frederique, et al. "Les Pactes Nationaux pour l'Emploi des Jeunes." *Travail et emploi*, no. 6 (1980): 15–62.

Perlman, Richard. *OJT in Milwaukee*. Milwaukee: Industrial Relations Research Institute, University of Wisconsin, 1969.

Perloff, Jeffrey, and Wachter, Michael. "The New Jobs Tax Credit: An Evaluation of the 1977–78 Wage Subsidy Program." *American Economic Review* 69 (1979): 173–179.

Perry, C.; Anderson, B.; Rowan, R.; and Northrop, H. *The Impact of Government Manpower Programs, in General, and on Minorities and Women*. Philadelphia: Industrial Research Unit, The Wharton School, 1975.

Pettman, Barrie O., and Fyfe, J., eds. *Youth Unemployment in Great Britain and the Federal Republic of Germany*. Bradford, England: MCB, 1977.

Piore, Michael J., ed. *Unemployment and Inflation*. White Plains, N.Y.: Sharpe, 1979.

President of the United States. *Employment and Training Report*. Washington, D.C.: Government Printing Office, 1980.

Public/Private Ventures. *The Impact of Pre-employment Services on the Employment and Earnings of Disadvantaged Youth*. Philadelphia: Public/Private Ventures, 1982.

————. *Private Sector Initiatives Program: Documentation and Assessment of CETA Title VII Implementation*. Philadelphia: Public/Private Ventures, April 1982.

Reubens, Beatrice. *Bridges to Work: International Comparisons of Transition Services*. Montclair, N.J.: Allanheld, Osmun, 1977.

————. *Policies for Apprenticeship*. Paris: OECD, 1979.

Reubens, B. G., Harrisson, J.A.C., and Rupp, K. *The Youth Labor Force 1945–1995: A Cross-National Analysis*. Totawa, N.J.: Allanheld, Osmun, 1981.

Reyhu, Lutz, et al., *Employment Policy Alternatives to Unemployment in the Federal Republic of Germany*. Translated by Eileen Martin. London: Anglo-German Foundation for the Study of Industrial Security, 1980.

Rist, R. D., ed. *Confronting Youth Unemployment in the 1980s*. New York: Pergamon Press, 1980.

Sartin, Pierette. *Jeunes au travail, jeunes sans travail*. Paris: Les Editions d'Organization, 1977.

Schwartz, Bertrand. *L'Insertion professionnelle et sociale des jeunes: Rapport au Premier Ministre*. Paris: La Documentation Française, September 1981.

Sellin, B. *Youth Unemployment and Vocational Training*. Berlin: CEDEFOP, 1981.

Serbein, Oscar. *Educational Activities of Business*. Washington, D.C.: American Council on Education, 1961.

Sherraden, M. W. "Military Preparation in a Youth Employment Program: The Civilian Conservation Corps." *Armed Forces and Society* 7 (1981): 227–245.

Sherraden, Michael, and Eberly, Donald. *National Service: Social, Economic and Military Impacts*. New York: Pergamon Press, 1982.

Shimada, Haruo. *The Japanese Employment System*. Japanese Industrial Relations Series. Tokyo: Japan Institute of Labour, 1980.

Sorkin, Alan. *Education, Unemployment, and Economic Growth*. Lexington, Mass: Lexington Books, 1974.

Sorrentino, Constance. "Youth Unemployment: An International Perspective." *Monthly Labor Review* 104 (1981): 3–14.

Spring, Joel. *Education and the Rise of the Corporate State*. Boston: Beacon, 1972.

Stevenson, Wayne. "The Transition from School to Work." In *The Lingering Crisis of Youth Unemployment*, edited by V. Adams and Garth L. Mangum. Kalamazoo, Mich.: W. E. Upjohn Institute for Employment Research, 1978.

Swedish Employers' Confederation. *Preparation for a Future*. Stockholm: Swedish Employees' Confederation, 1981.

Teresakeil, E., Riddell, D. S., and Green, B.S.R. "Youth and Work: Problems and Perspectives." *Sociological Review* 14 (1966): pp 105–120.

Tickner, Frederick. *Training in Modern Society*. Albany: Graduate School of Public Affairs, State University of New York, 1966.

Timpane, Richard, et al. *Youth Policy in Transition*. R–2006-HEW. Santa Monica, Calif.: Rand, June 1976.

Tokyo Electric Power Co. *A Policy for Human Resource Development*. Tokyo: Tokyo Electric Power, circa 1980.

Tsurumi, Yoshi. *Japanese Business*. New York: Praeger, 1978.

Tyack, David B., ed. *Turning Points in American Educational History*. New York: Wiley, 1967.

U.S. Chamber of Commerce. *A Survey of Federal Employment and Training Programs*. Washington, D.C.: National Chamber Forecast and Survey Center, September 1978.

U.S. Congress. House. Committee on Education and Labor. *Problems of Youth Unemployment*. Washington, D.C.: Government Printing Office, January 1980.

———. *Report on the Youth Act of 1980*. 96th Cong. 2d sess. Washington, D.C.: Government Printing Office, 1980.

U.S. Congressional Budget Office. *Improving Youth Employment Prospects: Issues and Options*. Washington, D.C.: U.S. Congress, February 1982.

———. *Youth Employment and Education: Possible Federal Approaches*. Washington, D.C.: U.S. Congress, 1980.

U.S. Department of Labor. *Profile of the Teenage Worker*. Bulletin no. 2039. Washington, D.C.: Government Printing Office, October 1980.

U.S. Department of Labor, Employment and Training Administration. *The National Apprenticeship Program*. Washington, D.C.: Government Printing Office, 1980.

U.S. Vice President's Task Force on Youth Employment. *A Review of Youth Employment Problems, Programs and Policies.* Washington, D.C.: Government Printing Office, 1980.

Van Lennep, Emile, and Marshall, Ray. "Le Chomage des jeunes." *Revue française des affaires sociales,* no. 1 (January–March 1978): 249–256.

Vernon, R., ed. *Big Business and the State: Changing Relations in Western Europe.* Cambridge: Harvard University Press, 1974.

Violas, Paul. *The Training of the Urban Working Class.* Chicago: Rand McNally, 1978.

Weir, A. D., and Nolan, F. J. *Glad to Be Out? A Study of School Leavers* Edinburgh: Scottish Council for Research in Education, 1977.

Wheatley, D. E. *Apprenticeships in the U.K.* Collected Studies Series, no. 3. Brussels: Commission of the European Community, September 1976.

Williams, Shirley, et al. *Youth Without Work: Three Countries Approach the Problem.* Paris: OECD, 1981.

Winterhager, W. D., et al. *Comparative Study of the Financial, Legislative and Regulatory Structure of Vocational Training Systems.* Berlin: CEDEFOP, 1980.

Woodrow Wilson School. *The Transition from School to Work: Report on the Princeton Manpower Symposium, May 9–10, 1968.* Princeton, N.J.: Woodrow Wilson School, 1968.

Youth Knowledge Development Report. *Research on Youth Employment and Employability Development.* Washington, D.C.: Youthwork, 1980.

INTERVIEWS

Federal Republic of Germany

Kurt Brandes, Bundesanstalt fur Arbeit
Dr. Ingrid Drexel, Institut fur Sozialwissenschaftliche
Dr. Echterholter, Budesministerium fur Arbeit und Sozialordnung
Mr. Freidberg, Abteilung Aus und Weiterbildung, Dynamit Nobel
Dr. Hurlebaus, Deutscher Industrie und Handelstag
Gero Lenhardt, Max Planck Institute fur Bildungsforschung
Dr. Manfred Leve, Bundesanstalt fur Arbeit
Dr. Leverkus, Bundesministerium fur Arbeit und Sozialordnung
Dr. Mannstetten, Bundesministerium fur Arbeit und Sozialordnung
Alfred Michler, Bundesanstalt fur Arbeit
Alexander Muller Reus, Siemens, A.G.
Gunther Schmidt, International Institute of Management
Burkart Sellin, CEDEFOP
Dr. Heinz Stegmann, Bundesanstalt fur Arbeit
Dr. Karl Joseph Uthmann, Bundesinstitut fur Berufsbildung

France

Mme. Robert, Délégation à l'Emploi, Ministère du Travail
Dr. Jean Rousselet, Director, Centre d'Etudes de l'Emploi

M. Schalchi, Ministry of Training
Dr. Bertrand Schwartz, University of Paris, Dauphine

Japan

Masao Aihara, Japanese Confederation of Labour (Domei)
Professor Ikuo Arai, Tokyo Institute of Technology
Osamu Hirota, The Japan Institute of Labour
Tokio Iinuma, The Tokyo Electric Power Co., Inc.
Dean Hideo Ishida, Graduate School of Business Administration, Keio University
Professor Kauo Koike, Kyoto Institute of Economic Research, Kyoto University
Yasuo Kuwahara, The Japan Institute of Labour
Tadashi Nakamura, Employment Policy Division, Ministry of Labour
Masaya Seo, Manager, Personnel Department, The Tokyo Electric Power Co., Inc.
Toshio A. Suzuki, Japan Federation of Employers' Associations (Nikkeiren)
Yasuo Suzuki, The Tokyo Electric Co., Inc.
Hisanori Yokodate, Japan Federation of Employer's Associations (Nikkeirren)
Koh Yoshino, Japan Federation of Employers' Associations (Nikkeiren)

OECD

Jarl Bengtsson
Chris Brooks
Ian Dawson
Carla Fasano
Ken Pankhurst
Peter Schwanse

Sweden

Birgitta Ahlkvist, Swedish Employers' Confederation
Kent Carlsson, Swedish Employers' Confederation
Tommy Wahlstrom, Swedish Employers' Confederation

United Kingdom

Mr. Barry, Economist, Manpower Service Commission
Mr. Dawe, Director of Special Programs, Manpower Services Commission
Mr. Elphinstone, Operations Section, Manpower Services Commission
Mrs. Glazier, Policy Section, Manpower Services Commission
Mr. Graystone, Trades Union Congress (TUC)
Ms. Legerton, Manpower Services Commission
Ms. Malloy, Department of Employment, Manpower Services Commission
Mr. Moorhouse, Corporate Affairs, Shell Oil
Ms. Pinschof, Head of Research, Manpower Services Commission

Mr. Reid, Manpower Intelligence and Planning Division, Manpower Services
    Commission
Mr. Robert, Confederation of British Industry (CBI)
Mr. Storrs, Manpower Services Commission
Mr. Vere, Confederation of British Industries Unit, Manpower Services Com-
    mission

United States

Charles Back, Director, Dutchess County Department of Employment
Joseph Ball, Manpower Demonstration Research Corporation
Burt Barnow, Department of Labor
Paul Barton, National Manpower Institute
Susan Grayson, Staff, U.S. Congress
Jane Herzog, National Alliance for Business
Kitty Higgins, Staff, U.S. Congress
Eileen Keefe, National Alliance for Business
Fritz Kramer, Department of Labor
Beatrice Reubens, Conservation of Human Resources Project, Columbia Uni-
    versity
Ann Rosewater, Staff, U.S. Congress
Elizabeth Clarke Smith, American Telephone & Telegraph Co.

Index

Aid to Families with Dependent Children (AFDC), 36
American Federation of Labor, 13, 16
American Federation of Labor and Congress of Industrial Organization (AFL-CIO), 115-26
apprenticeship, 23, 48, 62, 63, 77, 78, 95, 105, 109, 130
Areas Redevelopment Act of 1961, 30, 107
Association of German Chambers of Industry and Commerce (DIHT), 117
Ausbildungsplatzforderungsgesetz (Training Places Promotion Act), 108-109

baccalauréat, 20
Baccalaureat de technician (BTN), 21
Barton, Paul, 8
Berufsibildungsgesetz of 1969, 108
Berufschulen (German vocational schools), 23
Berufsfachschulen (German educational and vocational schools), 23
brevet de technicien (BT), 21
brevet d'études professionnelles (BEP), 21
Bundesansalt fur Arbeit, 63, 90
Bundesinstitut fur Berufsbildung, 64
Burns, Arthur, 31

career education, 25
Central Organization of Salaried Employees (PTK), 101

certificat d'aptitude professionnelle (CAP), 21
classroom training, 47, 105
collèges d'enseignement technique (CETs), 20
Committee for Economic Development, 57
Community Service (CS), 42
Comprehensive Employment and Training Act (CETA), 27, 29, 51, 96, 107-108, 115
compulsory school attendance, 103
Conant, James, 24
Concentrated Employment Program (CEP), 32, 50
Confederation of British Industries (CBI), 43, 117
Confédération Générale des Cadres (CGC), 119
Confédération Générale du Travail (CGT), 119
Confederation of Swedish Trade Unions (LO), 101, 118
Conseil National du Patronat Français (CNPF), 119
Cooperative Area Manpower Planning System (CAMPS), 33
cooperative education, 49

Denmark, 100
DIHT, 117
disadvantaged, 32, 44, 51, 95
Douglas, Paul, 30

About the Author

DAVID A. BRESNICK is Director of the Center for Management Development and Organization Research at Baruch College in New York City and a frequent consultant to government agencies in the United States and abroad. He is the author of *Managing Human Service Organizations in Hard Times* and *Public Organizations and Policy* and has written many articles for business and professional journals.